J. F. Purkis, B.A.
Principal Lecturer in English at Ware College

Assignments in communication

Longman London and New York

Longman Group Limited London

Associated companies, branches and representatives throughout the world

Published in the United States of America by Longman Inc., New York

First published 1980

British Library Cataloguing in Publication Data

Purkis, Joseph
Assignments in communication. – (Longman secretarial studies series).
1. Communication in management
I. Title
651.7 HF5718 79–40571

ISBN 0–582–41189–0

Printed in Great Britain by McCorquodale Newton Ltd.

Longman Secretarial Studies Series

Series Editor
A. R. Leal
Head of Business Studies Department, Plymouth College

Titles in the series:
Assignments in communication *J. F. Purkis*
Background to business *W. Owen and A. R. Leal*
Progressive transcription development *M. Quint*
Progressive typwriting assignments *M. Quint and A. Edwards*

Series foreword

I am more than pleased to note that the increasing popularity of the secretarial examinations of the London Chamber of Commerce and Industry, Commercial Education Scheme, has led to a publisher feeling justified in launching a series of books specifically designed to meet our syllabus requirements.

In 1956 the Commercial Education Scheme introduced a comprehensive and progressive scheme of secretarial qualifications which now range from the Secretarial Studies Certificates, through the Private Secretary's Certificate, to the high levels of the Private Secretary's Diploma. The standards were set high, but were a realistic interpretation of the demands by employers of their employees at different points in their careers. The success of this policy is seen in the increasing numbers of candidates from centres in the UK and overseas and with the very considerable public recognition by Press, Radio and Television when the Secretary of the Year Award is announced on the basis of the candidate achieving the best all-round success in the Private Secretary's Diploma.

May I wish all potential students every success, and hope that they and their teachers will find considerable help in this book.

R. W. Cattell, MA, FESB, MBIM
Director of the Commercial Education Scheme
London Chamber of Commerce and Industry

Preface

This book has been written for those concerned with business communications, for secretarial students on courses leading to the Certificates of the London Chamber of Commerce – the Certificate of Secretarial Studies, the Private Secretary's Certificate, the Private Secretary's Diploma – and for business students following BEC National Level Courses in 'People and Communications'.

It begins by assuming that the reader is familiar with the basic language skills of spelling, punctuation and grammar, and that she can use them to express her ideas effectively and adequately both in writing and in speech. She should also show that she understands the written and spoken communications of others by her own responses to them.

In Part 1 the emphasis is laid on the process of communicating with others in business. Part 2 examines the way in which business people express their understanding of others. Both parts offer examples of the various forms that are in use. In Part 3 the reader is presented with a collection of working situations out of which communication activities arise and which make use of the material that has appeared in the earlier part of the book.

I wish to thank those who have made this book possible – Mr. A. R. Leal, the General Editor of this series and my Head of Department, my colleagues in the Business Studies Department at Ware College and my students, many of whom have, unknowing, provided both useful ideas and constructive criticism. In conclusion, my appreciation and gratitude go to my wife for her continuing assistance and support throughout the writing of the book.

J.F.P.

Contents

Series foreword *iv*
Preface *v*

Part 1 **Business communication** 1

Introduction 1
Internal communications 1
The memo 1
Notices 4
Memoranda 8
External communications 12
The letter 12
Writing the letter – Seeking information – Giving information – Ordering goods and asking for services – Giving instructions – Praise or complaint – Letters replying to the correspondence of others
Telegrams and Telex 32
The telegram – Telex – Sending a Telex message
Reports 37

Part 2 **Understanding others** 41

Introduction 41
Basic comprehension 41
Listening 41
Reading 41
Recording, reporting and summarising speech 42
Verbatim reporting 42
Notes on what is said and done at meetings 43
Notice of meetings and agenda 45
The Annual General Meeting 45
An Extraordinary General Meeting 46
General Meetings 47
Board or Executive Meetings 48
The minutes of meetings 50
Annual General Meeting 51
General Meeting 53

Summary of correspondence 55
Summary in note-form 59
The synopsis, digest and abstract 63
Synopsis 63
Digest 63
Abstract 64
Charts and diagrams 64
Forms and questionnaires 67
Compiling forms 69
Compiling questionnaires 69
Completing forms and questionnaires 77

Part 3 Assignments in communication 79
Assignments 1–44 79

Index 154

Business communication

Part 1

Introduction

Effective communication is essential for all industrial, business and administrative activity. In this part communication will be considered from the viewpoint of those giving instructions, seeking information or making others aware of facts or ideas. In Part 2 the subject will be examined from the viewpoint of the receiver of information.

An examination of business practice shows that there are certain basic forms of communication. In this part we shall deal with the following:

1. Within an organisation – memos; notices; memoranda.
2. Between organisations, or between organisations and individuals – letters which seek information, give information, order goods or ask for a service, give instructions, offer praise or thanks, make complaints or are in reply to others; telegrams and Telex messages.
3. Reports – in letters or memorandum form.

Internal communications

THE MEMO

Within any organisation messages, requests for information or instructions are constantly being passed from one individual to another. Many of these are spoken, person to person, by telephone or by recorded message. In the course of a single day an individual may find herself receiving many different messages. There is, consequently, a risk that some may be forgotten. A wise secretary will make appropriate notes. Those who constantly send messages will be aware of this tendency towards forgetfulness and so send written messages to ensure that their communications are remembered. The word 'memorandum' means 'something to be remembered'. A lengthy document was called a 'memorandum'. Where there was more than one such document, or a document having more than one point, the plural form 'memoranda' was employed. These terms are still in use. When the material to be remembered was much shorter the abbreviated form 'memo' came into use.

A memo then is a short document, usually about one topic, sent by one person within an organisation to others in the same group. Quite frequently, because the messages are short, memos are written or typed on smaller sheets of paper. In many organisations pads of specially prepared memo forms are used.

The following Examples (1–3) illustrate the layout and contents of memos. These examples do not have a title indicating the name of the organisation. This is because memos are brief, internal documents and it is unnecessary to refer to the organisation's title.

Example 1

MEMO

To: Section Leaders of the Accounts, Sales and Secretarial Sections. **Date:** 15th March, 1980

(Copy to: General Manager, Oldbridge.) Reference: O/Adm.3.

From: The Chief Accountant

Invoice Serial Numbers.

The Company has opened a branch at Oldbridge.

The serial numbers of all invoices issued by the Oldbridge branch will be prefixed by the code letter O.

E.g. O/BS 2138.

Serial numbers of invoices issued here at Head Office will continue to have no prefix.

Notes to Example 1

1. Each memo must indicate clearly the names or status of the people for whom it is intended.
   In this example the memo is sent to the Section Leaders concerned with Sections dealing with Invoices at Head Office. A copy is being sent to the General Manager at Oldbridge to let him know that the information has been circulated at Head Office.
2. The name or status of the sender must be stated.
3. *Date.* All documents should indicate the date when they were composed or issued.
4. *Reference.* If it is intended that any document is to be kept for future

reference, the reference number of the file in which the sender's copy is kept should be quoted.
Not all memos, however, need to be filed away. (See the next example.)

5. *Subject title.* This should be a very brief summary of the nature of the contents of the memo.
6. *Subject matter.*
   (*a*) This should be expressed as briefly and clearly as possible.
   (*b*) It must be related to the subject title and not include irrelevant matter.
   (*c*) If there is to be more than one topic use separate headings. (See Example 3, given below.)
   (*d*) Each new point made in connection with the topic should be given a fresh paragraph.
7. If the sender is named at the beginning it is not usual for the memo to be signed or the information repeated. Occasionally, one may find a memo with the sender's initials typed in, especially if his status only has been given.

Example 2

MEMO

```
To: Janet.                                  Thurs. Sept. 7th
From: Mr. Smith.                            11.00 a.m.

I have been called away suddenly to meet the Managing Director at
the Manchester Office.  Will you phone my wife and let her know that
I shall not be home until late this evening?

                                            J.S.
```

Notes to Example 2

1. As Janet, Mr. Smith's personal secretary, was absent when he was called away, he left her a memo.
2. This memo does not need to be filed. Once the instruction has been carried out it may be thrown away.
   For this reason:
   (*a*) the year is not given in the date, but the time is given to indicate when Mr. Smith was about to leave;
   (*b*) no reference number is given;
   (*c*) no subject title is given.
3. The message itself is clear and concise.
4. Mr. Smith has made the message more personal by giving his initials at the end.

Example 3

MEMO

To: All members of staff. 7th January, 1980.
From: The Managing Director. **Ref:** JHB/Pers.80/1.

Mr. John H. Smith, M.B.E.

We were all very pleased to learn this week of the award, mentioned in the Queen's New Year Honours List, of the M.B.E. to our General Manager, Mr. John H. Smith. This has been given in recognition of his very valuable services to the St. John Ambulance Brigade.

On behalf of all members of Newtown Electrical Products, Ltd., I offer him our very hearty congratulations.

Miss Agnes Smiley.

Miss Smiley has been appointed Deputy General Manager of our Southampton branch from February 1st this year. We congratulate her and offer her our good wishes for the future.

Notes to Example 3

1. This is a memo which contains more than one topic.
2. In each part the writer has been informative. He wished the whole staff to know the facts. He also sought to identify himself with the staff in offering good wishes. In doing both of these he has still managed to keep the message brief and simple.

NOTICES

Notices are not addressed to any specified persons but are intended for all who may be in a position to read them. They must be designed to attract the reader's eye and be put in suitable places.

The design of a notice depends upon its contents and its purpose. A notice may give a warning, convey instructions or evoke a response from its readers. In a large multi-storey car park there is always a risk of theft. It has been decided that notices should be put up, the wording to read, 'Take care! Thieves like this car park. Protect your property. Lock your car'. What size of notice should be used? How should the message be presented? What colours should be used?

Having designed a suitable notice, where should it be placed? At the back, behind the cars? On the pillars? At the entrances and exits? At what height?

In most organisations notices are displayed on notice-boards or affixed to walls, but the same principle applies – they must be seen.

The following Examples (1–3) are of notices intended for public display.

Example 4

SAVE ENERGY —
SWITCH IT
OFF.

Notes to Example 4

1. This notice should be printed in large bold letters.
2. It will be more effective if placed immediately above the switch panel on a wall.

Example 5

NOTICE

USE OF STATIONERY

ALL members of staff are asked to observe the following rules for the use of stationery.

1. Do not use memo pads for rough notes.
2. The Company's headed note-paper is not to be used for private purposes.
3. When typing letters staff should take only one copy unless a special request is made for more.
4. Please keep carbons stored flat and away from radiators.

Notes to Example 5

1. This notice will be affixed to the door of the stationery store, to all notice-boards in all offices and elsewhere.
2. The subject heading, 'Use of Stationery', should be made to stand out clearly.

3. Consideration should be given to line spacing in order to achieve the maximum impact.

Example 6

NEWTOWN DOMESTIC PRODUCTS

Are YOU interested in the EXPORT of OUR products?

Would YOU like to follow one of our famous NEWTOWN FREEZY-COOKER UNITS from our factory to its new home in the European People's Palace on the Adriatic Sea in YUGOSLAVIA?

The chance could be yours.

Early in May the management will arrange for FOUR of its staff to follow the unit, No. NT201468, on every stage of its journey. The lucky four will start here as they see it loaded into one of NEWTOWN DOMESTIC PRODUCTS large vans. They will go with the van to the Container Section at Tilbury Docks. Arrangements have been made for the four to be taken on a conducted tour of the Container Depot there. They will accompany the container with the Unit No. NT201468

- on the ferry
- by road across Europe

to the People's Republic of Yugoslavia where they will become the guests of the European People's Palace. They will witness the unloading of the container and the movement of our unit to the European People's Palace where they will see it installed. For two complete days they will stay at the Palace, after which they will fly home to Newtown.
ALL THIS WILL COST NOTHING.

If you are interested you can get a form* at the staff shop when you purchase £2 worth of goods. Complete the form and return it to the staff shop for ballot by March 21st, 1980. The first FOUR forms taken out of the ballot box will entitle their holders to follow our FREEZY-COOKER UNIT.

* ONE only per employee.

Notes to Example 6

1. This notice appeared on all the company's notice-boards at the beginning of February 1980.
2. The heading indicates that it was issued by the company.
3. It is addressed to all company employees.

4. Notice how the use of **you** and the question mark is designed to make every reader personally involved.
5. The section giving details of the journey is set apart by being indented from the left margin.
6. An effective notice must indicate what action is to be taken. In this, instructions are given:
   (*a*) to get a form – at the staff shop;
   (*b*) to return the form to the staff shop – by a certain date.
   This notice also indicates the method by which the four will be chosen.

The above are notices intended for display on walls or notice-boards. Copies of Example 6 could also have been distributed to the company's staff. Sometimes, notices are prepared for distribution rather than for exhibition on a notice-board.

Example 7 was distributed in employees' pay envelopes and Example 8 was printed and sent out in bundles to each section head for distribution.

Example 7

INCOME TAX DEDUCTION.

The tax changes announced by the Chancellor of the Exchequer in his Autumn Budget have been included in this week's/month's pay envelope. The changes include increases in allowances for married men and single persons and the increased level at which the basic rate is paid. Personal tax codes have been changed. You should have received details from the tax office. This week's/month's pay includes the tax rebate due because of backdating to April 6th. If you have any queries, the Wages and Salaries Accounts Section will try to help you.

Notes to Example 7

1. This notice concerns everyone because it relates to earnings and tax.
2. It briefly summarises what has been done.
3. It indicates where advice can be obtained if needed.

Example 8

Notes to Example 8

1. This notice is intended for all members of staff.
2. Sufficient information is given to enable individuals to decide whether or not to accept the invitation.
3. Clear instructions on action to be taken are given.

NEWTOWN ELECTRONICS DEVELOPMENTS LTD.

Once again the invitation is given to all members of the staff to attend the Annual Dinner/Dance, which will take place on Friday, November 30th, from 8.00 p.m. to 2.00 a.m.

We are very fortunate in being able to have the Fitzwilliam Room at the Grand Hotel, Newtown.

Three choices of menu are available; table wines will be provided by the Chairman of the Company. Those who intend to be present are asked to indicate their choice of menu on the attached slip. Details of the menus may be seen on the notice-boards.

During the evening two bands will be in attendance, the Newtown Supremes and the Hopeshire Gondoliers. The bar adjacent to the Fitzwilliam Room will be open until 1.00 a.m.

If you wish to accept this invitation will you please complete the slip and return it to the General Manager, via your section manager, not later than Friday, August 31st?

Following the practice of previous years, each member will be allowed to bring one guest.
June 30th, 1980.

To: The Managing Director, Newtown Electronics Ltd.

I shall be attending the Annual Dinner/Dance at the Grand Hotel, on Friday, November 30th.
I *shall/shall not be bringing a guest.
I would prefer Menu *A/B/C.
My guest would prefer Menu *A/B/C.

Signed.

Section.

*Please delete what is not required.

4. The detachable slip provides the means for the reply to the invitation.

MEMORANDA

From time to time new ideas, new schemes, new situations, new processes emerge.

Consider the following situations:

1. A manufacturing firm finds that a bottleneck in production is reducing output.

The chief production engineer examines the situation. Having studied the factory layout and the machines, and having consulted the operatives he concludes that a rearrangement of the layout and some modifications in the machinery are needed. These involve structural changes in buildings, and the retraining of some employees; they will also be costly. The results of his enquiries will have to be set out in a well-argued document, duplicated and sent out to all those involved. He may compose the document himself or delegate the task to a competent personal secretary or deputy. The presentation of his ideas in a document enables the points to be remembered and recalled as they are being discussed.

2. A company specialising in the sale of electrical goods throughout the country finds the results in one area very disappointing. An investigation reveals personality clashes and that some sales representatives are unsuitable and are unaware of the company's sales techniques and policy. As a result the managing director at Head Office sends out two documents. The first, to area sales managers, deals with personnel management and the problems of sales representatives. The second restates company policy and techniques and is intended for the sales representatives.

These two situations illustrate the types of written documents that have to be produced to enable business administration and progress to take place. The two documents that result from these situations, much longer than memos or notices, are known as **memoranda**. One document is called a memorandum.

Example 9

Hopeshire and South-East Garages Ltd.

MEMORANDUM

FROM: The Managing Director. **Date:** August 31st, 1980.
TO: All Branch Managers. **Reference:** HO/MD/PS 4.

Forecourt Sales - Losses Procedure.

In recent weeks each branch has reported losses in the accounts of the forecourt sales sections. These losses are quite serious and considerable. I am sending this memorandum to ask all managers and all staff to take every possible step to prevent this. The following procedures should be put into operation.

1. KEEP ALERT AND OBSERVANT.
Some losses are caused by downright dishonesty and theft. Where goods are out for sale assistants are asked to keep a watch for pilferers and petty thieves. If staff have reason to suspect anyone they must send for the manager or some other senior person to investigate. If necessary, suspects should be taken to the manager's office and held there until the police arrive.

The heaviest losses come from non-payment for petrol. If a driver is seen to fill his car and to attempt to drive away without paying for it, the registration number of the vehicle and such other details that can be obtained should be noted and reported at once to the manager. A note should also be made of the grade and amount of the petrol taken. The police must be informed at once.

Whenever possible there should be an attendant on duty on the forecourt to assist customers needing help and to be able to provide the information that will help in the detection of thieves.

The last major form of dishonesty arises from fraudulent use of cheques and banker's cards. Procedures to be followed to help to lessen loss in this way are given in the next section.

2. PAYING FOR PETROL AND OTHER ITEMS.
a) It is the policy of the Company to sell petrol at the price indicated on the pumps. It takes into account any reductions from recommended prices.
b) As our garages operate on the self service principle cashiers will be working from a console in an office or kiosk. When dealing with a customer it is important to ensure that the correct petrol meter is being read.

c) PAYMENT for petrol and goods sold on the forecourt may be made in one of the following ways:
(i) by cash,
(ii) by cheque,
(iii) by Access or Barclaycard.
In all cases the amount must be recorded on the cash register and the customer issued with an official receipt.

d) PAYMENT BY CHEQUE.
(i) All payments by cheque must be guaranteed by a banker's card. Each kiosk or office has a leaflet indicating which cards are acceptable. Please check that the card is valid - that it has not expired and that it has been signed.

(ii) Cheques must be made payable to 'Hopeshire and South-East Garages Ltd.'

(iii) On the reverse side of the cheque the following information should be entered:
- complete credit card account number,
- the customer's address,
- for petrol sales - the customer's car registration number,
- the cashier's initials.

(iv) Compare the signature on the card with the one on the cheque. If in doubt, send for the manager.

(v) No cheques may be accepted for sums in excess of £50. In this event payment must be made by cash or credit card.

e) PAYMENT BY CREDIT CARD.

Only 'Access' and 'Barclaycard' are acceptable. If payment is by credit card this procedure is to be followed:

(i) The caution list is to be consulted. If the customer's name or card number is on the list the manager must be sent for and a note made of the customer's car registration number. If the name is not on the list the transaction may proceed.

(ii) A check must be made that the card is not time-expired and is signed.

(iii) The appropriate machine must be used to impress the customer's card details on the relevant voucher.

(iv) On the voucher must be entered:
- date, branch number, cashier's initials,
- details of sale - each item separately stated and priced. The number of gallons and grade of petrol must be given and the customer's car registration number must be entered,
- the total value of the items.

(v) If the total should exceed £50, confirmation for the transaction must be obtained from the Barclaycard or Access Centre which will give a code number to be entered on the voucher.

(vi) When the details have all been entered, the customer should sign in the required space. The top copy and the firm's receipt should be given to him and his card returned to him. The remaining copies will be placed in the cash register in the cheque section.

Notes to Example 9

1. This memorandum would probably be printed on the company's own headed paper, and at least one copy sent to each garage.
2. The word 'Memorandum' indicates the nature of the document.

3. Remember the rules: for whom is it intended?
   who is sending it?
4. Both date and reference number are essential.
5. *Title* – a short title. It gives:
   (*a*) a reason for the document – 'Forecourt Losses'; and
   (*b*) a way of stopping them under the heading 'Sales Procedure'.
6. The opening paragraph expands the first half of the short title, 'Forecourt Losses'. It also makes it clear that what follows is to be acted upon.

   In the rest of the memorandum the managing director calls for careful vigilance and gives precise details of acceptable methods of payment for petrol and other goods provided on the forecourts.
7. At all times ensure that what is written is clear and concise.

External communications

THE LETTER

The business forms considered so far are those in common use within an organisation. For external communications the letter is more usual. It is distinguished by its special layout.

Example 10 is an illustration of the layout used when a single individual sends a letter to another person or organisation.

Example 10

Notes to Example 10

1. Address of the sender is on the right-hand side, at the top. It is not usual to put the sender's name here.
2. Give the date when the letter was composed. The student should note the following forms:
   7th February, 1980
   February 7th, 1980
   7.2.80.
   Of these the first is preferred.
3. *Inside address.* This gives the name and address of the person or organisation to whom the letter is being sent. Whenever possible the letter should be addressed to a person – e.g. The Manager, The Personnel Officer, The Principal.
   Some organisations prefer to put this address after the letter, but still on the right-hand side.
4. *Salutation – opening.*
   (*a*) When the person addressed is referred to by an office use
   Dear Sir, or Dear Madam,
   Dear Sirs, or Dear Mesdames.

14 High Rd.,
Newtown, **1.**
Hopeshire,
NE7 2AJ.

7th February, 1980 **2.**

The Manager,
Newtown General Stores,
3. Market Lane,
Newtown,
Hopeshire, NE7 4BC.

4. Dear Sir,
I have just received your Spring Offers leaflet and am very interested in your special freezer packs.
5. I am enclosing a cheque for £5. Will you please send me two of these packs?

I am,
Yours faithfully, **6.**
Enc. Janet Tomkins. **7.**

(*b*) When the addressee is referred to by name it is permissible to use that name:

Dear Mr. Jones, or
Dear Miss Smith.

5. *The message.*
6. *Closing salutation.*
   (*a*) When opening forms given in 4(*a*) have been used, the closing salutation should be 'Yours faithfully'. Some people still use 'Yours truly'.
   (*b*) When the opening forms given in 4(*b*) have been used, the closing salutation is 'Yours sincerely'.
   (*c*) The author's analysis of letters received from business and administrative correspondents shows that there is a tendency to use 'Yours sincerely' on most occasions, irrespective of whether or not the more formal forms of opening address have been used.
7. *The signature of the writer.* If there is any doubt about the identity of the writer or the writer's status, the writer should clarify this. In the form: I am,

   Yours faithfully,
   J. Tomkins

   there is no indication of (*a*) the writer's sex
   (*b*) the writer's status.

As far as sex is concerned there is a tendency in most cases to assume that 'J. Tomkins' is Mr. J. Tomkins. A reply envelope will be so addressed. In the above illustration this may be remedied by writing:

(*a*) J. Tomkins
MISS J. TOMKINS, MRS. J. TOMKINS
MS. J. TOMKINS. or

(*b*) by signing Janet Tomkins as in the specimen letter given in Example 10.

In the specimen letter given in Example 10 the writer's status is not necessary. The correct practice will be indicated in letters given below.

Many organisations prefer to use headed stationery. Example 11 is an example of such a letter.

Example 11

1. **NEWTOWN INDUSTRIAL ENTERPRISES LTD.**
28–32 Stephenson Drive, Newtown, Hopeshire NE8 5SS.
NEWTOWN 68234. (STD Code 0029.)

Our reference: ACCOUNTS DEPT.
Your reference: CHIEF ACCOUNTANT'S SECTION.
(Ext...............).

7th February, 1980 2.

H.M. Inspector of Taxes,
Newtown,
Crown Buildings,
3. High Street,
Newtown,
Hopeshire, NE7 1PQ.

4. Dear Sir,

PAYE TAX TABLES 5.

Would you please send me two more complete sets of tax tables for use in the Wages Department? 6.

Yours faithfully, 7.

J. Y. Money. 8.
(CHIEF ACCOUNTANT) 9.

Notes to Example 11

1. *This is headed notepaper.* Its layout is determined by the management. It will provide for the title of the organisation, its address and telephone number, spaces for filing references and space to indicate which department or section is sending the letter.
2. *The date.* Although the example given shows the date in the traditional position on the right side, some organisations may place the date elsewhere – for example, more to the centre of the page. In this, as in so much else, the practice of the organisation should be followed.
3. *Name and address* – of the person or organisation receiving the letter. See notes on previous example given.
4. *Opening salutation.* See notes on previous example.
5. *Title.* This short title is an indication of the nature of the letter's subject matter. It is an aid to filing and reference.
6. *Message.*
7. *Closing salutation.* See notes on previous example.
8. *Signature.* See notes on previous example.
9. *Authority of sender.* In the previous example it was stated that the status of the sender should be shown. It is helpful practice to indicate this after the signature.

WRITING THE LETTER

So far, in this section, attention has been given to the format and layout. The most important part of the letter is the message, to which we shall now turn.

Seeking information (Example 12)

Example 12

Notes to Example 12

1. *Format.* The writer is enclosing an envelope and has written **Enc** (= enclosure) at the bottom left-hand corner of the letter. The figure '1' follows to show that there is only one enclosure. In business correspondence it is standard practice to type this in whenever any extra documents are enclosed in the envelope.
2. *Content*

   Para. 1. Writer briefly introduces himself and his purpose in writing. **Para. 2.** He seeks information about Forestry camping sites. He begins with a general request and follows it by asking for information on specific points. In this letter these points have been listed separately under each other. **Para. 3.** He states that he is enclosing a stamped addressed envelope.

27 Alberry Avenue,
Newtown,
Hopeshire,
NE7 8QT.

February 26th, 1980

The Site Administrator,
The Forestry Commission,

Dear Sir,

I am the leader of the Mornington Lane Youth Club, Newtown, whose members wish to camp for two weeks in August, 1980.

I understand that the Forestry Commission has a number of sites set aside for camping purposes. I should be very pleased if you would send me further details about these sites. I would like the following information:

a) where they are situated
b) what kind of camping is allowed
c) what the costs are per person per week
d) if there are any vacant sites during the month of August, and
e) what must be done to book the site.

I enclose a large stamped addressed envelope for reply.

I am,
Yours faithfully,
Robert Wright.

Enc. 1.

Giving information

In the next example Dr. K. W. Brightman has previously accepted an invitation to speak to students at Newtown College of Technology and Art on 'Computers in industry'. He has written to the Principal for information about the type of students to be addressed, what audio-visual aids are available and how to get to the College. This letter (Example 13) gives the Principal's reply. It will be sent on College headed notepaper.

Example 13

Notes to Example 13

Para 1. A brief acknowledgement of Dr. Brightman's letter. **Para 2.** This answers Dr. Brightman's query about the audience – the number, their department, their experience of computer studies. **Para. 3.** The Principal makes clear what visual aids will be available and where. He also offers the services of a technician. **Para 4.** Outline of route from

NEWTOWN COLLEGE OF TECHNOLOGY AND ART
FARADAY AVENUE, NEWTOWN, HOPESHIRE NE1 3SS.

PRINCIPAL: A. M. NEVINGTON-NEWNES, M.A., M.Sc.(Econ.).

November 18th, 1980

Dr. K. W. Brightman, F.R.S., M.Sc.,
Head of Dept. of Industrial Technology,
North-Western Polytechnic,
Cumberside.

Dear Dr. Brightman,

Visit to Newtown College of Technology & Art.

I was delighted to receive your letter of November 15th, concerning your visit to us on December 12th.

I estimate that you will have an audience of 200 students drawn from the Technology, Computer Science and Business Administration Departments. They will be pursuing courses leading to either BEC Higher Level or Degrees in their respective studies. All will be familiar with the groundwork of Computer Studies, including Programming and Data Processing.

The Audio-Visual Aids officer has been instructed to provide a 16mm sound film projector and a remote-control slide projector to hold a rotary magazine. These will be in the main lecture theatre where screens will be set up ready for use. The A.V.A. officer has promised that a technician will be available.

You state that you will be travelling by car down the M1. As you approach the London area you should look for the A448 exit to Newtown. Follow this route for some 40 miles. There are two exits from the A448 into Newtown. If you follow the second it will take you to the Town Centre complex. The College is on the right-hand side of this.

We have had some sketch maps printed showing the location of the College in relation to the Town Centre and other major roads. I enclose one for your guidance.

When you reach the College come to the main gate. A porter will be on duty to direct you to the Car Park and from there to the main administration building. The entrance to my secretary's office is on the right as you enter. She will bring you to me.

I hope you will find these instructions of use in helping you to get here. We are all looking forward to your visit.

Yours sincerely,
A. M. Nevington-Newnes.
(PRINCIPAL)

Enc. 1.

M1 to Newtown Town Centre and College. **Para. 5.** A map is enclosed. **Para. 6.** Information on reception at the College. **Para. 7.** Short paragraph to conclude letter. This letter is lengthy but nothing in it is irrelevant to the topic of Dr. Brightman's visit.

Ordering goods and asking for services

Those who order goods or ask for services to be performed must make their instructions as clear as possible. Vagueness and ambiguity waste time and money because they lead to further letters or telephone calls which could have been avoided.

Attention should be paid to the following:

(*a*) Have the correct quantities been ordered?
(*b*) Have the articles been referred to by the correct names? (Bolts and screws are different and some people are vague when identifying materials.)
(*c*) Are the appropriate descriptive words being used? Colours need checking.
(*d*) Is there a code or reference number which needs quoting?
(*e*) Are the manufacturer's or supplier's conditions being observed? For instance, has postage to be added?
(*f*) Has the sender any special instructions that will save time and trouble later?

Examples 14–16 are examples of this type of letter.

Example 14

12 High Street,
Newtown,
Hopeshire.

November 19th, 1980

The Manager,
Bright Goods Ltd.,
Oldchester,
Oldshire.

Dear Sir,

Will you please send me a copy of your mail order catalogue as advertised in 'The Daily Echo', dated November 18th, 1980?

I am,
Yours sincerely,

Elisabeth Jones (Mrs.)

Notes to Example 14
This is a simple example of an individual's request for a catalogue. The article ordered is identified as a 'mail order catalogue'. The writer further identifies it by referring to an advertisement in a newspaper.

Example 15 is an example of a letter used by a company for ordering numerous goods.

Example 15

WONDER TOYS MANUFACTURING COMPANY LTD.,
12–18 Cumberland Way, Newtown, Hopeshire.

Please reply to: The Office Manager.
November 28, 1980

The Manager,
Paperchase Ltd.,
Times Lane,
Oldchester,
Oldshire.

Dear Sir,
Would you please supply the undermentioned goods to us at the above address and charge them to our account?

20 reams ''Angel Bright'' white duplicating paper, A4 size
10 reams ''Paperchase'' white flimsy paper, Quarto size
10 reams ''Paperchase'' pink flimsy paper, Quarto size
6 boxes ''Replica'' carbon paper, black, Quarto size
1,000 White envelopes 6'' x 4'' - gummed
500 White envelopes 6'' x 4'' - ''Eezi Seal''
1,000 White foolscap envelopes.

Yours faithfully,

Office Manager.
(J. Tomkinson.)

Notes to Example 15
1. The company's headed note-paper has been used.
2. Quantities of each item ordered are set out under each other in one column.
3. Brand names are indicated in inverted commas.
4. Stationery is being ordered – colours and sizes are necessary to cost

it. If the costing is included it should be set out so that a total of separate items may be made.

Example 16 is an example of a letter which includes costing.

Example 16

THE ENGLISH OIL COMPANY

Head Office: Petrol House, Centre Street, Newtown.

English Oil Wharf,
Dock Lane,
Oldchester,
Oldshire.

September 8th, 1980

The Manager,
Popular Calendars Ltd.,
High Street,
Newtown.

Dear Sir,

I wish to order the items listed below. Will you please send them to me at the above address at Oldchester?

48	1981 Calendars ''English Industries''	
	Ref. PC6/81 @ £1.20 each	57.60
10	''Popular'' Day at a Glance Desk Diaries	
	Ref. PC5/81 @ 95p each	9.50
24	Planning Diaries - Long size	
	Ref. PC4/81 @ £1.30 each	31.20
	Total	98.30

I understand that orders over £20 are sent carriage paid. I enclose a cheque for £98.30.

Yours faithfully,

Enc. 1. W. Tanner (Branch Manager.)

Notes to Example 16

1. In the opening instructions the writer makes it clear to which of the two addresses the goods are to be sent.
2. Three columns are given – one for quantity, one for description and price of each item and one for costing that part of the order.

3. Under description the writer describes the item and then helps to identify it by use of the appropriate reference number. This is followed by a statement of the cost for each item.
4. When ordering goods and enclosing cash, the writer should check on requests for addition of postage and packing, insurance and VAT.
5. One enclosure.

The next letter (Example 17) is a request for a service. Here it is important that the exact nature of the service is given.

Example 17

The English Oil Company

English Oil Wharf,
Dock Lane,
Oldchester,
Oldshire.

October 25, 1980

The Manager,
Oldchester Garages Ltd.,
Testing Lane,
Oldchester,
Oldshire.

Dear Sir,

Servicing and Maintenance of Vehicles.

In accordance with this Company's agreement with you I would like you to make arrangements to carry out the following items of servicing, maintenance or testing.

Servicing.

Registration.	Vehicle.	Type of Service.	Observations.
JKL 686K	Ford Transit Van	6,000 mile	Engine sluggish in starting
PSO 211L	Fiat 128	Major Service	Check suspension.
PSD 459H	Escort 1300	Extended Service	Windscreen wipers not working.
LSD 268R	Ford Ghia De Luxe	6,000 mile	Check lighting.

Maintenance.

GVV 474S Vauxhall Chevette. The steering on this vehicle has been giving trouble.

ABC 215F Ford Cortina. Respray and rust treatment.

Testing.

The following vehicles are due for an M.O.T. on the dates indicated.

ATW 326F	November 8.
SSG 211L	November 10.
1 HW	November 15.

Will you please let me know when you can take these vehicles?

Yours sincerely,

J. F. Carr.
(Transport Manager)

Notes to Example 17

1. *Subject heading.* This indicates briefly the nature of the services required.
2. The service required falls under three headings and the letter is divided accordingly.
3. Vehicle registration numbers are provided because the garage books all work in by reference to name of customer and his vehicle number.
4. In detailing the work required the writing has been kept down to a minimum although there is enough to enable the garage staff to estimate the time that might be required.

Giving instructions

Many job advertisements bring a quick and large response which necessitates spreading the interview of applicants over several days. Each will receive a letter calling her to the interview and giving clear instructions concerning the procedure to be followed.

Example 18 is an example of such a letter.

Example 18

Notes to Example 18

1. *Subject heading.* This refers to the vacancy to be filled.
2. *Opening paragraph* – acknowledgement of application and general plans for dealing with all applicants.

Smith, Jones and Atkins Ltd.

4–10 Sunshine Lane, Newtown, Hopeshire.

Personnel Office.
October 4, 1980

Mrs. J. K. Johns,
1 Adam Lane,
Oldbridge,
Hopeshire.

Dear Mrs. Johns,

Post of Office Supervisor, Accounts Section.

Thank you for your letter of application for the above mentioned post. Arrangements have been made to interview applicants on Tuesday and Wednesday, November 6th and 7th.

Will you please arrange to attend at 10.15 a.m. on Tuesday, November 6th?

Will you please arrive at 10.00 a.m. and report at the reception desk? You will then be brought to my office.

You should bring with you the original certificate giving proof of your examination successes and evidence of your membership of any professional bodies.

It is the policy of the company to refund any expenses incurred in coming to this interview. A form of application for this purpose is attached. You should complete this and hand it to my secretary before you leave.

Will you please inform me whether or not you will be attending the interview?

Yours sincerely,

V. Goode.

Enc. 1. Personnel Officer.

3. The rest of the letter consists of a number of instructions to Mrs. Johns. Each paragraph deals with a different instruction: to attend on a certain date – reporting on arrival – evidence of qualifications – refund of expenses – request for Mrs. John's decision about attendance.
4. All instructions to be brief, but try to vary form in which they are expressed.

Praise or complaint

Most people, at some time, have to praise others for good service or outstanding achievement. When doing this in writing, especially in business, one must avoid the charge of insincerity caused by being too effusive or excessive in the use of vocabulary.

On the other hand, when criticising or complaining it is important to avoid the impression of rudeness or unfairness. The facts upon which criticism is based should be stated clearly and accurately. Whenever possible, in assessing motives or behaviour, the complainant should give the benefit of the doubt to those being criticised. For instance, if a parcel does not arrive, one should not make the charge, 'You did not send it', but rather write, 'So far I have not received the goods that I ordered', or 'I should like to know if you have despatched the goods that I ordered'.

In what follows the reader will find examples of letters offering praise or making complaint.

(a) Letter of praise (Example 19)

Example 19 (see opposite)

Notes to Example 19

1. This is an internal letter of praise and thanks. The message of the Board's gratitude is first expressed in the decision to ask the Managing Director rather than the Secretary to write to Mr. Jones.
2. The facts on which the praise is based are set out.
3. This is a business achievement and the praise is expressed in business terms: 'drive' – 'efficiency' – 'loyal' – 'co-operation' – 'support'.
4. Sincere thanks are offered. The pleasure of the Board passed on. All who should be praised are involved.
5. The absence of excessive language avoids any suggestion that the Board is patronising.

(b) Letter of thanks (Example 20)

Example 20 (see page 26)

Notes to Example 20

1. Many people have experiences which, at the time, seem distressing. The writer of this letter also met with kindness and help. A letter of thanks in a situation such as this is always helpful.
2. The facts were recounted as simply as possible.
3. The writer has chosen to send the letter to a person senior to those involved. It has given her a chance to say her thanks and to make favourable comments about the staff at Upreach.
4. The General Manager wrote to the lady and he also sent a message to the Upreach branch. The second message is given in Example 21.

NEWTOWN ELECTRONICS

Head Office: 1 Faraday Lane, Newtown

From: The Managing Director.
26 June, 1980

Mr. J. L. Jones,
Manager,
Oldbridge Branch.

Dear Mr. Jones,

Sales Success - Oldbridge.

At its meeting today, the Board of Management of Newtown Electronics has been examining the sales returns from the various branches. The secretary drew the members' attention to the following facts:

1) The sales of the Company's products at Oldbridge Branch has exceeded those of any other branch, in terms of the number of articles sold.
2) The income from the goods sold at Oldbridge during the past three months is double that for the preceding three months.
3) The amount of outstanding debts for goods supplied at Oldbridge is being reduced.
4) Over the past year the only staff changes have been caused by retirement of three and by the marriage of one of the staff.

The Board is very pleased with the Oldbridge Branch, and has asked me personally to write to you.

The results are a tribute to your drive and efficiency and to the loyal spirit of co-operation and support of your staff.

Will you please accept my sincere thanks and convey the pleasure of the Board to all who work at Oldbridge Branch?

Yours sincerely,

James L. Hope.
Managing Director.

12 Lindsey Drive,
Newtown,
Hopeshire.

24 October, 1980

The General Manager,
Newtown Universal Stores,
High Street,
Newtown, Hopeshire.

Dear Sir,

On Thursday, while shopping at the Upreach Branch of your stores in Newtown I suddenly realised that the pendant and chain which I had been wearing were missing. The store was packed and I had little hope of seeing the items again. However, I spoke to an assistant at the glassware counter. She called for the store manager. He and other members of the staff were so helpful that when I left the store I felt that everything possible had been done.

I was most surprised to receive, on the Friday morning, a packet containing the missing items. They had been sent by the Manager, who informed me that one of the cleaners had found them on the floor beneath a counter.

I am writing to you to tell you how thankful I am to have recovered these items.

The staff were most helpful and friendly. In addition, it is very encouraging to find that people can be honest and hand in items which they find.

Will you please give my thanks to all who had been so helpful to me?

Yours faithfully,

Jayne Goldcrest.
(Mrs.)

Example 21 (see page 27)

Notes to Example 21

1. Copying machines make it easy to provide copies of correspondence.
2. It is good for morale that a communication of this kind and also the thanks of the management are passed on to those concerned.

(c) Letter of complaint about goods

In the last few decades there has been an increase in mail order selling.

Newtown Universal Stores

High Street, Newtown, Hopeshire

From: The General Manager.
27 October, 1980

To: The Manager,
Upreach Branch,
Newtown.

Dear John,

I am sending you a copy of a letter I have received from Mrs. Goldcrest concerning her chain and pendant.

I am delighted to receive letters like this. It is obvious that you and your staff have made a good impression. Experiences of this type help to build up the good name of the Company.

Please give my thanks to all concerned.

Yours sincerely,

Enc. 1.

Jeffrey Jansen.

Goods so ordered do not always come up to our expectations on arrival or develop weaknesses after they have been used for a time.

There has also been a rapid increase in the number of mass-produced items and the speed of production leads to some articles being offered for sale which are unsatisfactory.

Most sales organisations or manufacturers recognise that goods may prove to be faulty and will provide for customers to return items for refund, repair or replacement. Whatever the customer chooses, his letter should make it clear that it is a complaint. The nature of the fault should be clearly stated, details of the purchase outlined and the desired remedy indicated.

Example 22 (see page 28)

Notes to Example 22

1. Heading – this refers to machine about which a complaint is being made.
2. The first paragraph briefly refers to details of purchase. This enables the suppliers to check information and decide if the machine is still under guarantee.
3. The next paragraph indicates that faults have developed. No criticism or blame is allocated. In the early part the reference to operators is a way of saying that you do not think they are to blame.

Newtown Universal Stores
High Street, Newtown, Hopeshire

The Equipment Section.
July 24th, 1980

The Manager,
Business Products Ltd.,
High Street,
London EC3.

Dear Sir,

Business Products Duplicator, No. BP 79/4189.

In April your company delivered to us the duplicator referred to above. It was accompanied by your invoice, reference number BP 79/6048, dated April 17th, 1980.

Since it has been in use these faults have been reported by the operators, all of whom have attended the special course of instruction on duplicators, arranged by you.

1. The automatic paper feed sometimes misses or it delivers about 15 sheets at a time.
2. The paper counter is not functioning.
3. When the machine is being operated automatically far too much ink is being supplied to the rollers.
4. On four occasions the fuse has blown.

As the machine is still under guarantee I should be pleased if you would send a mechanic to investigate and remedy these faults. I would like this done as soon as possible as the company is having to use an old, slow, hand-operated model.

Yours faithfully,

T. Williams.
Equipment Officer.

The faults are clearly outlined.

4. Reference to guarantee – followed by a request for speedy action.

(d) Letter of complaint about service

It is not only goods that may prove to be faulty. Sometimes they have to be installed, or maintained, or even removed, all of which require the services of others. Their work is usually satisfactory, but occasionally the unexpected happens. People who have promised to call fail to do so. The gas cooker is not repaired to our satisfaction; the car engine still has that irritating rattle. We make phone calls to the companies concerned only to find that the operator who answers fails to

Example 23

Newtown Universal Stores

High Street, Newtown, Hopeshire

The Equipment Section.
August 25th, 1980

The Manager,
Business Products Ltd.,
High Street,
London EC3.

Dear Sir,

Business Products Duplicator, No. BP 80/4189.

On July 24th, 1980 I wrote to you about the above mentioned duplicator. In my letter I drew attention to a number of faults that had been reported and I requested that a mechanic be sent to investigate and remedy them in accordance with your guarantee.

Since then I have heard nothing further, although I would at least have expected an acknowledgement of my letter.

On August 7th I telephoned and was told by the operator that no trace of the letter could be found. She suggested that I ring the following day when you or your deputy would be available. I did so and spoke to Mr. Adams whom I understand to be your Assistant Manager. He did find the letter and promised to send a mechanic.

On August 16th I made another phone call and was told that the mechanic was booked down to visit Newtown Universal Stores that week. He has not arrived.

I am most disappointed that no action has been taken in spite of my statement that we are having to use an old, slow, hand-operated model, and in spite of your firm's promise by phone.

I should be very pleased if you would treat this as a matter of great urgency and arrange for the mechanic to call within the next 48 hours. Will you please advise me at once by phone that you have done so?

Yours faithfully,

T. Williams,
Equipment Officer.

Notes to Example 23

1. Heading. This repeats the heading used on the letter to which reference has been made.

2. The first paragraph briefly summarises the contents of that letter.
3. The next two paragraphs outline telephone action taken on two occasions.
4. Paragraph 5 summarises the writer's reaction to the lack of response.
5. The last paragraph contains a further request for action but it is put more strongly than it was in the previous letter.
6. The last sentence, although an instruction, is expressed in the grammatical form of a question. The question mark should be used.

---

understand our problem and is unable to find someone who does. She promises to ring back, but forgets. It is these situations that lead us to write the letter of complaint about the service that has been given or has not been received.

The letter, where possible, should be addressed to the person most likely to offer satisfaction. It should contain a statement of what was originally wrong, what action was taken to put it right and what is the writer's present complaint. The fact must be stated clearly and concisely. After this the writer should indicate what further action is expected. However exasperated or irritated one might be, her letter should be as courteous as possible.

Letters replying to the correspondence of others

The composition of letters is frequently a two-way process. Many of the letters that are sent from person to person, or from one institution to another demand a reply. The same is true of the letters that we receive.

In this section the reader will be reminded of some rules concerning letters of reply.

1. Unless the circumstances clearly permit otherwise all letters should be acknowledged. Sometimes it is not possible to deal with the matter of some letters at once. If there is to be a delay the one who receives a letter must state that the letter has been received and that it will be dealt with later (see Example 24).
2. The reply should first:
   (*a*) acknowledge that the correspondence has been received; and

---

Example 24

Notes to Example 24

1. Mr. Smith's letter is acknowledged.
2. The query cannot be answered at once, but a further reply is promised when Universal Stores gets the information.

Newtown Universal Stores

High Street, Newtown, Hopeshire

From the General Manager.
August 28th, 1980

Mr. S. W. Smith,
46 Cater Terrace,
Bridge-upon-Sea,
Hopeshire.

Dear Mr. Smith,

Thank you for your letter of August 24th in which you enquired if Part No. 2X.CZ1. can be used in the Universal Electronic Shears.

This question has not been raised before and it will be necessary for me to consult the manufacturers.

As soon as I receive a reply from them I will write to you again.

Yours sincerely,

Harry Johnson,
General Manager.

(*b*) identify the nature of the correspondence by referring where possible to its date, the subject title and the sender's reference code.

For example:

(*a*) Dear Mr. Jones,

I have received your letter of August 24th, 1980, concerning the vacant post of Assistant Accountant and thank you for it. or

(*b*) Dear Mr. Jones,

Thank you for your application of August 24th, 1980, for the vacant post of Assistant Accountant. or

(*c*) Dear Mr. Jones,

Appointment of Assistant Accountant

Thank you for your letter of application for the above mentioned post, which was dated August 24th, 1980.

3. Once the acknowledgement has been made the letter itself should be dealt with paragraph by paragraph, point by point.
4. After this has been done any additional matter or information relevant to the subject under discussion may be introduced.
5. It is not necessarily advisable to introduce completely new and non-relevant matter. If, however, it is decided to do so, the new matter should be introduced under a clearly marked heading.

The following (Example 25) is an example of a letter of reply. It is sent in response to the letter sent by Mrs. Jayne Goldcrest, to the General Manager of Newtown Universal Stores on 24th October, 1980 (Example 20).

Example 25

Newtown Universal Stores

High Street, Newtown, Hopeshire

28th October, 1980

Mrs. J. Goldcrest,
12, Lindsey Drive,
Newtown,
Hopeshire.

Dear Mrs. Goldcrest,

Thank you for your letter of 24th October, 1980, concerning your lost pendant and chain, which we were able to restore to you.

It is a pleasure to receive letters such as yours from grateful customers.

I have sent a copy of your letter to the manager of Upreach branch, together with a request that your message is made known to all concerned. I have also added my own words of appreciation.

Yours sincerely,

Harry Johnson.
General Manager.

TELEGRAMS AND TELEX

Before the coming of the modern era the process of communication was very slow indeed. Today, it is very different. As a result of radio and the telephone it is now possible for us to begin to communicate at one moment and our message be received a few seconds later in places thousands of miles away. Arising out of these developments two forms of business communication have come into being – the telegram and the Telex.

The telegram

This enables messages to be sent very rapidly from one person or organisation to another in any part of the world.

Three stages are involved:

(*a*) the person sending the message, or telegram, passes it to the nearest post office;
(*b*) that post office passes the message to the post office nearest to the person receiving the message;
(*c*) the second post office arranges for the person to whom the message is sent to receive it.

Of these three (*b*) is carried out by the use of the telephone or by radio. The other two stages may be slower. If the sender has no telephone he will have to go in person to a post office. Similarly, if the receiver has no telephone, the post office will have to arrange for someone to deliver the message.

The post office charge is related to the number of words contained in the message. The more words used the higher will be the cost. It can thus be seen that, in the interests of economy, the number of words should be kept to a minimum. To achieve this a number of conventions have developed in the composition of telegrams.

1. The sender gives the minimum information about herself – enough to enable the receiver to identify her. Normally the post office asks for the sender's name and address but will *not* send it.
2. The name and address of the receiver should be kept to a minimum, enough to allow the message to reach its destination.
   If the full name and address reads:
   Mrs. Hilary Jones, 'The Heights', 14 Sable Crescent, Newtown, Hopeshire,
   the following will suffice for the telegram:
   Jones 14 Sable Crescent Newtown Hopeshire.
   The name. Surname is normally enough. Give more only if confusion might arise.
   The address. Omit the house name if street number is shown.
   Town and county. Normally the post office will ignore the county, unless there is more than one town of the same name in different parts of the country.
   Punctuation. Will not be used unless requested; in which case, each punctuation mark will count as a word.
3. Most businesses have arranged with a post office to have a telegraphic address, usually consisting of not more than three words.
4. *Punctuation.* The reference made to punctuation in note (2) above applies generally to the telegram. Any single punctuation mark will be charged for as a word. Each mark so charged will appear in a telegram as a word.
   e.g.: I have understood stop everything in order
   or: I have understood. Everything in order.

A general rule is that punctuation marks should be omitted where possible but used if it is necessary to avoid misunderstanding.

e.g.: Number sold each day last week 76 comma 77 comma 78. . . .
or: Seventy six seventy seven seventy eight.

5. *The message.* From all that has been said above it is clear that inessential words should be omitted. The following examples will illustrate how telegrams should be written.
Message in full: I have arrived safely. I arrived at 7.28 this evening. The hotel is pleasant and comfortable. John Smith.
Telegram: ARRIVED SAFELY 1928 GOOD HOTEL JOHN
Situation: Mike Driver has been testing his racing car, Angel II, on the Isle of Man. It has developed trouble and he needs to fit a new exhaust before he can test again. The race for which he has entered is in three days' time. It is a special exhaust made only by the manufacturers of the car, Britspeed Autos, of Manston, in Kent. He decides to send a telegram requesting a replacement to be flown to Ronaldsway Airport, near Douglas. The firm have been backing him for the race.
Telegram: Addressed to BRITSPEED Manston.
Message: MOST URGENT REQUIRE NEW EXHAUST UNIT ANGEL II FLY TO RONALDSWAY WILL COLLECT MIKE DRIVER

Note

(i) All telegram messages are received printed in capitals.
(ii) MOST URGENT – emphasises need for very quick action.
(iii) REQUIRE NEW EXHAUST UNIT ANGEL II – it is not necessary to repeat events leading up to request. It is important to state what is wanted – UNIT implies all parts related to exhaust. Reference to ANGEL II will enable Britspeed to identify special parts.
(iv) FLY TO RONALDSWAY – firm will recognise Ronaldsway as the airport for the Isle of Man.
(v) WILL COLLECT – indicates that Mike Driver will go to the airport.

Reply telegram: Addressed to DRIVER QUEEN'S HOTEL DOUGLAS.
Message: EXHAUST ON WAY CESSNA GB121 ARRIVING 1930 RONALDSWAY GOOD LUCK BRITSPEED

Note

(i) EXHAUST ON WAY – Britspeed indicate that part required has been despatched.
(ii) CESSNA GB121 – Aircraft carrying it identified.
(iii) ARRIVING 1930 – Time of arrival given so that Driver can collect.
(iv) RONALDSWAY – Airport confirmed.
(v) GOOD LUCK BRITSPEED – Appropriate greetings.

Telex

Telex is basically an extension of the telephone. When one speaks into the mouthpiece of the telephone the spoken sounds are converted into electrical impulses which are transmitted through the system along cables or as radio waves. By operating the appropriate dial number the sender arranges that these impulses are received at the other end by a similar piece of machinery and then reconverted into human and other sounds. It is then possible for those at either end to carry on backwards and forwards conversation.

In the Telex system the speaking and listening pieces at either end are replaced by specially constructed typewriters. At the sender's end a message is typed out and can be read like any typed message. When the dialling mechanism has been operated so that the apparatus at the other end is brought into action the typed message is converted into electrical impulses as the typing proceeds. These are transmitted in the same way as other 'phone messages and at the receiving end are converted back so that an identical message is printed. This process means that a message being typed at one end can be read almost simultaneously at the other.

The speed at which a message is received is related to the speed of typing by the sender and the capacity of the apparatus to work at that speed. In many firms there is a further refinement of the system in that the typed message is converted into punched tape which can be fed through the system at a faster rate. This is useful, especially over long distances, because the cost of sending Telex messages is related to the telephone costs – i.e. to time and distance.

Sending a Telex message

1. Before she begins to send out any Telex message the operator should ascertain the dialling code and answerback of the person with whom she wishes to communicate. If she is going to communicate via the operator, of if those to whom she is sending her message are overseas she should find the appropriate operator's overseas codes.
2. The next stage is to set the apparatus in motion by pressing the button marked 'DIAL'. When the apparatus is ready a green light will show.
3. Dial the appropriate code. When the number has been connected the operator will have printed on her typewriter the answerback of the other end. She should check that it is the one she wants.
4. If it is the correct one the operator must send her own answerback code – either by pressing the button marked 'HERE IS' or by typing it.
5. The message should then be sent.
6. When the message is finished the operator should send her answerback and then ask for the other person's answerback by pressing the key 'WHO ARE YOU' for a short time.

7. She should then follow the close down procedure – ten line feeds. Press the button marked 'CLEAR' and wait till the green light goes out.

These instructions are intended for use with internal automatic Telex communications in Britain. Those who wish to communicate manually, via the operator, or who wish to communicate with overseas correspondents, should consult the instructions issued for the guidance of Telex operators by the post office.

The following is an example of the layout of a typical Telex message:

889999 NEWTOWNELECT
779696 OLDBRIDGE – LIGHTS.
1130 APL 24TH ATTN MR. WILLIAMS.
CAN YOU PSE SEND TWENTY NEWTOWN BAR FIRES FIFTEEN NEWTOWN 2KW BRIGHTFIRES TEN SOFTHEAT UPRIGHT FIRES ASAP SUDDEN RUN CAUSED BY WEATHER PRICE AND DELIVERY ADVICE PSE
REGARDS SWEETMAN

779696 OLDBRIDGE LIGHTS

Notes

1. 889999 NEWTOWN ELECT. Dialling code and answerback of receiving exchange.
2. 77969 OLDBRIDGE LIGHTS. Dialling code and answerback of sending exchange.
3. The message. All letters are in capitals:
   (*a*) ATTN: PSE: ASAP – these are examples of standard and acceptable abbreviations which should be used where possible.
   (*b*) *Times*. These should be expressed according to the 24-hour clock.
   (*c*) *Content*. A study of the above message will show it to be a compromise between the telegram and letter forms. The severe telegram form is not necessary as the sender is not paying for each word transmitted. Instead he pays for the time he is using on the telephone system. Unnecessary words, such as articles and some verbs, can be omitted. On no account should material essential to the message be left out.
   The message when composed, should leave no room for misunderstanding or confusion.

889998 NORTHSEA MOTORS LOND.
779659 NORTHSEA MOTORS BORDER.
1530 MAY 17 ATTN MR. WOODS.
WEEKLY SALES RETURN W/E MAY 15TH.
MAY 9 A 518 B 464 C 291 D 100
MAY 10 A 609 B 418 C 320 D 98
MAY 11 A 550 B 424 C 285 D 102

MAY 12 A 499 B 446 C 276 D 113
MAY 13 A 523 B 471 C 259 D 84
MAY 14 A 586 B 432 C 314 D 118
MAY 15 A 595 B 441 C 331 D 97.
JOHNSON

779659 NORTHSEA MOTORS BORDER

Notes

1. This is an example of a Telex message sent by a branch of a chain of garages to Head Office. It is a weekly sales return.
2. Once again standard abbreviations are used. attn. w/E.
3. Layout. To an outsider this Telex may not convey much meaning. It is a regular internal communication. The letters mean:
   A – 4 star petrol
   B – 3 star petrol
   C – 2 star petrol
   D – Paraffin.
   The numbers that follow represent the number of gallons sold.

REPORTS

General Manager: 'Mr. Jones, The District Council Surveyor, has called an open meeting to outline the Council's proposals for the development of a new Industrial Estate in the South-East corner of the town. I would like you to go along and hear what he has to say and then let me have a report. You can get all the details from my secretary'.

Throughout business and administration men and women are asked to make enquiries and carry out investigations, attend meetings, conferences and discussions and study various schemes and proposals. Sometimes they are given authority to act on behalf of their employers, or those who instructed them. When they have completed their task or mission they are expected to explain what has happened. Sometimes this account is presented orally but more frequently it is presented in a written form, which is known as a **report**.

Although this may be given in the form of either a letter or a memorandum, the main body will follow a standard pattern.

1. *The terms of reference.* In this part of the report the writer outlines the instructions that have been given to him.
2. *Method of attack.* An indication will be given of the action taken to carry out the instructions. This will refer to documents consulted, places and sites visited, objects examined and people interviewed.
3. *Findings.* These are presented in an orderly and systematic way. Sometimes a chronological order may follow; at other times the report will be presented under topic headings.
4. *Conclusions reached.* This section will follow an investigation of the findings.

10 Church View,
Oldchurch,
Hopeshire.

26th May, 1980

Dear Sir,

Accident involving a Volkswagen and a Cortina
on May 23rd, 1980.

I have been asked by Mr. Jones, of High Rise Hill, Lynsdown, to write to you about the accident referred to above.

I was standing outside the Europa Stores, Newtown High Street, Newtown, at the bus stop, waiting for the 1.15 p.m. bus to Oldchurch. A few minutes before the bus was due a red Volkswagen car, registration number XYZ 999S, was moving in the direction of Oldchurch, and approaching the bus stop. It was driven by Mr. Jones. He had no other passengers and did not appear to be travelling fast.

There is a turning on the other side of the road. Suddenly a blue Cortina, SJH 777L, drove from the turning at speed. It turned to the left but came out too far before attempting to turn. As a result it hit the rear of the Volkswagen and caused it to swerve round before it stopped. The Cortina continued to the edge of the kerb where it came to a halt.

Both drivers were shaken but managed to get out of their cars. The police were called.

Mr. Jones saw me at the bus stop and asked me if I had seen the accident. I said I had and at his request gave him my name and address.

The following day he rang me at my home and asked me to send you this account of what happened.

If you want any further information I will gladly let you have it.

Yours faithfully,
John Brown.

Name and address of the
Insurance Company.

5. *Recommendations.* Some investigations will reveal a need for further action. The writer may have been asked to consider this. If so, he will conclude the report by making his recommendations.

Some very formal reports may use these headings or ones similar in meaning. The reader will be able to examine some examples of report writing below.

One of the commonest types of report is about an event in which one has been involved or which one has witnessed. Example 26 is a letter report to an insurance company acting on behalf of a driver involved in a road accident.

Example 26 (see page 38)

Notes to Example 26

1. The underlined heading gives a brief summary of the subject of the report.
2. The first paragraph is a brief statement of terms of reference.
3. This report is intended to be a statement about an event.
4. No action was necessary. The result of the report is therefore a presentation of the findings – the statement of what happened.

The Wellingford Computer Company has had a staff social club for many years. The staff have been complaining that it is a waste of time and money because nothing ever happens. The committee members complain of lack of support. A new assistant accounts manager has been recently appointed and has been asked by the general manager to have a look at the situation and come up with some new ideas. He would like these in the form of a report. Example 27 is the result.

Example 27

To: The General Manager. Date: 27th March, 1980
From: The Asst. Accounts Manager. Ref: ETJ/SOC/80/1.

Report. Wellingford Computers' Social Club.

Shortly after my appointment in January, 1979, you spoke to me about the state of affairs of the Social Club and asked me to investigate.

I began by talking to the officers of the Social Club. At their suggestion I attended a meeting of the club committee. I decided after this to circulate a questionnaire to the staff. A copy is attached as an appendix to this report. About 60% replied to it, about half a dozen expressing their views quite strongly. I invited them to meet me and enlarge upon their criticisms and ideas.

Findings.

1. The Committee.

   There is a committee of eight men, all appointed at least four years ago. The youngest is 40 years old. No regular meetings are held. If the chairman or secretary wish to discuss any activities one of them goes to each committee member in turn to find out what he thinks.

2. Activities.

Every year there is a Christmas Dinner which is held in the staff canteen. In March the Annual Dinner/Dance is held. This is held at the public hall. The hall's catering staff provides the dinner and the 'Gently Soft' Dance Band provides the music for dancing, which is of the ballroom type, and 'old-fashioned' in the words of most members. The Christmas dinner is provided by the management and is well attended. About 25% of the staff attend the Dinner/Dance. The Committee say that this low attendance suggests there would be no response to other activities.

3. Comments of Members.

An examination of the questionnaire and conversations with the club membership has revealed:

a) there has been no effective communications between the committee for some time;
b) there is a desire for a new committee which should be representative of the members with regard to section, age and sex;
c) there would be support for a more varied and vigorous programme. Suggestions for the latter included dances to suit the younger members, theatre visits, sports sections;
d) support for the view that the management should help to provide suitable club premises;
e) members would be willing to pay an annual membership subscription to provide a better programme.

Recommendations.

1. The Wellingford Computers' Social Club should have a new constitution. This can be brought about under the existing rules by the President (the Managing Director of the Company) calling an extraordinary general meeting as soon as possible and offering a suitably worded agenda.
2. The new constitution should provide for a new management committee and officers.
3. An annual subscription of £2 should be proposed.
4. The new committee should be encouraged to work out a programme which will be supported by the membership.
5. The Company's Board should give consideration to the possibility of providing premises or rooms for club use.
6. Within their limits the existing committee have done their best. They should not go unthanked.

Finally, I would add that I am willing to co-operate with the President and the present officers in drafting a suitable agenda for the extraordinary general meeting.

ly, put an enc
vileges etc.) [F
tion (æbəlíʃə
g || (esp. *hi.*
lavery **abolítio**
L. *abolitio* (*a.*

Understanding others

Part 2

Introduction

The communication process involves sending out messages, but unless the receiver reacts in the appropriate manner the communication will be in vain. This part will help the reader examine communications from the receiver's viewpoint.

Basic comprehension

The first rule in understanding others is to pay attention carefully to what is said or written.

LISTENING

A listener must give her full attention to all the words spoken, trying to relate them to the ones that follow. She must clear her mind of all other thoughts. It will also help if she watches the speaker's lips and gestures. Sometimes understanding can be improved by asking a speaker to repeat or explain what has been said or by making written notes.

READING

It is usually possible to read a passage more than once. The reader should read it once to get the gist of it. A re-reading ought to enable her to give an oral account of the contents, including all main ideas.

Once this has been done the reader should check the vocabulary used and satisfy herself that she has grasped the meaning of all the words used, checking any about which she is uncertain.

1. A dictionary should be consulted where the reader is meeting words for the first time.

2. Sometimes words are used figuratively. The writer may try to convey meaning by making comparisons and using various kinds of image. If this kind of language is used the reader must be sure that the writer's meaning is clear.
3. It is useful to look out for idiomatic use of words and phrases. The latter may consist of two or three words. The meaning of the group is found by examining all the words together.
   For example:
   (*a*) This company has been *in the red* for some time. The phrase in italics is an idiomatic way of saying that the company's accounts have shown a debit balance.
   (*b*) She has not been *on form* lately. The phrase in italics means that the person concerned has not been maintaining her usual level of achievement.

A good reader will not be satisfied with a vague understanding of a writer's message. Having understood the vocabulary and diction (use of words) she should check the structure of the sentences and pay attention to the punctuation used.

Recording, reporting and summarising speech

A visitor to any organisation's offices will soon discover a considerable volume of written communication, but will also come to appreciate the significance of the spoken word. She will hear new ideas and schemes being discussed, decisions and agreements being made, and instructions being transmitted. The constant ringing of the telephone bell will remind her that this spoken communication extends beyond the buildings in which she finds herself.

In the following sections the processes of understanding the spoken word and of helping others to do so will be considered.

VERBATIM REPORTING

The management of National Domestic Supplies has been meeting to consider the effect that certain national industrial disputes are having on the company. The following (Example 28) is a word-for-word report or record of what was said in the first part of the meeting. Such a report is called a **verbatim** report.

The verbatim report is used particularly in circumstances where it is necessary to record exactly the words that have been spoken. Verbatim reporting is used for:

- proceedings in Parliament;
- court proceedings;
- public enquiries of various kinds.

Private firms and organisations will decide when such reporting is needed.

Example 28

GENERAL MANAGER: Ladies and gentlemen, I have asked you to meet me here this morning so that we can find out from each other the effects that the current national industrial disputes are having on the company and then consider any action that we might need to take. Mr. Jones, would you begin by telling us how the purchasing department has been affected?

MR. JONES (Manager of Purchasing Department): Certainly. I will first deal with the Seamen's strike. As you know, this will, tomorrow, be going into its second week. Three days ago we should have had from Germany a large consignment of washing machines, dishwashers, food mixers and blenders, and other goods for the home and kitchen. They are still in Germany because the German seamen and dockworkers are acting in sympathy with our seamen. If the strike goes on for another week our main stores will be unable to make up the stocks of our depots in the south-east, Manchester, Liverpool and Scotland.

The transport drivers' work-to-rule in this country has prevented the delivery to our Scotland depot of supplies from Sew-machines Ltd., and from British Kitchenware Supplies. Neither of these firms can give us a date for delivery.

GENERAL MANAGER: Thank you, Mr. Jones. Perhaps Mr. Johnson can fill in the picture concerning the Transport Section.

MR. JOHNSON (Transport Section Manager): If the Seamen's strike continues, my drivers will become idle at the end of next week. If it were not for the transport work-to-rule this would be a good time to give our vehicles a thorough service and overhaul. Unfortunately, the transport drivers' action is preventing us from getting some vital spare parts. As you know, the transport drivers have been preventing the tanker drivers from leaving their depot in the south-west and in Scotland. Until they can get out we shall be short of diesel and petrol.

....

NOTES ON WHAT IS SAID AND DONE AT MEETINGS

It is, however, more common to take notes of what is said and done at meetings or in conversation.

The following notes (Example 29) might have been taken at the above meeting.

Example 29

```
Management meeting - Oct. 25th 1980.
Called to consider effects of strikes and industrial action on
company.  Also possible action.

Effect on Purchasing.

a) Seamen's strike  - second week.
                    - holding up consignment of domestic,
                      electrical goods from Germany.
                    - will affect stocks S.E., Manchester,
                      Liverpool and Scotland.
b) Transport drivers - affecting deliveries to Scottish depot from
                       Sew-machines Ltd. and British Kitchenware.

Effect on Transport Section.

a) Seamen's strike - drivers becoming idle
   Transport drivers - lack of spares making servicing and
                       overhaul work difficult.
                       Drivers action holding up delivery of spares.
                     - interfering with supplies of petrol and
                       diesel in S.E. and Scotland.
                       Could be short.
```

The following points should be noted.

1. At meetings and discussions each person tends to jot down points that he or she may consider useful.
2. This example (29) might be the notes made by the General Manager. These can be duplicated to serve as reminders of points made.
3. In this example speakers are not named but, where appropriate, their sections are.
4. Complete grammatical sentences are not given but the points recorded must be understood by those who were present.
5. *Layout.* The notes are presented under the heading of the effect on each section. Each industrial action is considered in turn.
   An alternative presentation could be:
   (*a*) Seamen's strike.
   Effect on purchasing ....
   Effect on transport ....
   (*b*) Transport drivers' action.
   Effect on purchasing ....
   Effect on transport section ....

Whatever the type of organisation, public or private, their rules specify that business and other activities should be discussed, agreed upon and authorised on fixed occasions and according to a set programme. These fixed occasions are called **meetings**. In the non-public organisations – charitable and voluntary organisations – the meetings of all members are called **General Meetings**. The annual meeting which considers the accounts, elects new officials and debates resolutions is called the **Annual General Meeting**. Sometimes, however, it may be necessary to request a special meeting to consider some special or urgent business. This is an **Extraordinary General Meeting**.

After election, the officers and committee members will meet together at frequent intervals to run the organisation. In companies these may be known as Board or Management meetings: in other organisations the more usual terms are Committee or Executive Committee meetings.

One of the officers, usually the Secretary, calls these meetings and informs the members of the business to be discussed. She does this by sending them a **Notice of Meeting** and an **Agenda**, that is a list of items to be discussed.

Notice of meetings and agenda

THE ANNUAL GENERAL MEETING (Example 30, page 46)

This example (30) is a typical Notice of Meeting and Agenda. The wording and format will be determined by the organisation's rules and by law. Limited companies, for example, are governed by various Companies' Acts which specify, among other things, that a certain time must elapse between the sending out of a notice of meeting and the meeting itself. Some bodies allow business to be raised that is not on the agenda; others forbid discussion of anything not on the agenda.

Members of annual general meetings are usually presented with an account of the previous meeting, referred to as the **minutes** of the meeting. In addition a report is given on the result of any transaction mentioned in these minutes.

The Chairman's report informs members of the business and policy of the organisation over the past year and possibly of future plans. Similarly, the organisation's financial progress is also reviewed in the presentation of the accounts, which have usually been examined and checked by an independent auditor. Each of these reports may be subject to questions and discussions. The members will then be asked to accept or reject them. The latter is effectively a vote of no confidence.

NEWTOWN ELECTRONICS COMPANY LTD

Coronation Drive,
Newtown,
Hopeshire.

1st April, 1980

Dear Sir, or Madam,

Annual General Meeting of Shareholders.

Notice is hereby given that the 10th Annual General Meeting of Newtown Electronics Company Ltd. will be held on 24th May, 1980, at the Newtown Civic Hall, in the Queen's Room, starting at 5.30 p.m.

The Agenda of the meeting is given below.

Yours faithfully,

L. V. Sparks.
Secretary.
Newtown Electronics Co. Ltd.

AGENDA

1. Minutes of the 9th Annual General Meeting of the Company.
2. Chairman's Report.
3. Presentation of the Audited Accounts and Balance Sheet.
4. Appointment of Officers and other members of the Board.
5. Appointment of Auditors.

The other important activity at the annual general meeting is the appointment of officers, members of the Board (or Committee or Council) and auditors. These will act in the name of the company or organisation for the ensuing year. The names may be proposed by the Board or nominations may be invited from members. In the latter event due notice will have been required of nominees so that voting forms may be prepared and despatched to all members.

If the rules permit any other matters to be included in the agenda of the annual general meeting this may be submitted either by the Board or by other members.

AN EXTRAORDINARY GENERAL MEETING (Example 31)

In this example (31) the meeting was called following action by members. In most organisations the Management or Executive

HOPESHIRE COUNTY PRESERVATION SOCIETY LTD

10 Linnet Drive,
Newtown,
Hopeshire.

30th May, 1980

Dear Member,

Extraordinary General Meeting.

In accordance with the relevant Companies Acts and the Society's Articles of Association I have been requested by fifty members to call an Extraordinary General Meeting.

This will be held at the Newtown Civic Hall, in the Queen's Room, on Friday, 29th June, 1980 at 7.00 p.m.

The Agenda is given below. Members are reminded that the rules do not allow the raising or discussion of any other business at this meeting.

Yours faithfully,
Alan F Bird.
Secretary.

AGENDA.

1. To consider proposals for building a permanent headquarters and exhibition building at the Hopeshire Marshes site.
2. If the proposals are accepted, to appoint a Marshes H.Q. Building sub-committee.

Committee, the Board or the Council also have the right to call such a meeting.

GENERAL MEETINGS (Example 32, see page 48)

General Meetings are organised like Annual General Meetings, the notice of meeting being followed by the Agenda (see Example 32).

The business to be discussed will be decided by:

(*a*) the previous minutes. In this agenda the secretary has drawn attention to two items. It is open to members to ask about other items;

(*b*) the Committee, or Council, of the Society;

(*c*) members who give sufficient notice of an item.

Apart from the minutes and business arising from them, the other items on the agenda are normally matters that the Committee has

HOPESHIRE COUNTY PRESERVATION SOCIETY LTD

10 Linnet Drive,
Newtown,
Hopeshire.

30th June, 1980

Dear Member,

General Meeting.

The Summer General Meeting of the Society will be held at the Oldchurch Community Centre on Friday, 20th July, 1980, at 7.30 p.m.

The Agenda for the meeting is given below.

Yours faithfully,
Alan F. Bird.
Secretary.

AGENDA.

1. Minutes of the General Meeting held on Friday, January 19th.
2. Business arising from the minutes.
   a) Proposed Oldchurch By-pass.
   b) Sandy Marsh scheme.
3. Correspondence: Letter from Chairman, Hopeshire County Council Planning Committee.
4. Chairman's Report.
5. Financial statement for first quarter.
6. Proposals for Marina at Seabridge and its effects on Hopeshire Marshes.
7. County Survey of Butterflies.
8. Other Business. Notice of motions or topics should be given to the Secretary not later than Friday, July 13th.
9. Date and place of next meeting.

already discussed and considers important enough to bring before a full meeting. The Chairman's report will enable reference to be made to less important matters.

BOARD OR EXECUTIVE MEETINGS

To carry out day-to-day business smaller groups (the Board of Directors, Board of Management, Council, Committee, Executive Committee) are appointed to act on behalf of the larger group. Each consists of the officer, Chairman, Secretary and Treasurer, and a number of others without specific duties. Their functions may include:

(*a*) keeping a record of membership;

Example 33

NEWTOWN ELECTRONICS COMPANY LTD.

Coronation Drive,
Newtown,
Hopeshire.

June 5th, 1980

Dear ,

Board of Management Meeting - June 12th, 1980

The monthly meeting of the Board of Management will be held on June 12, 1980, at 10.00 a.m. in the Board Room.

The agenda is given below.

Yours sincerely,
L. V. Sparks.
Secretary.

AGENDA.

a) Minutes of meeting held on May 15th, 1980.
b) Business arising.
   i) Application to join National Association of Electronics Producers.
   ii) Annual dinner-dance.
c) Correspondence.
   i) Letter from ACAS concerning allegation of sex-discrimination against female radio assemblers.
   ii) National Appeal - Youth Venture Scheme.
d) Monthly accounts report.
   Mr. Clarke will be reporting progress in clearing bad debts.
e) Departmental Reports:
   i) Management and Secretarial:
      a proposal will be made that the Company changes to electric typewriters.
   ii) Accounts Section:
      the effect on accounts staff of the Chancellor's recent Budget proposals.
   iii) Transport Section.
   iv) The Factory: request for wage increase by assembly workers.
f) Flexitime: the Personnel Officer will outline details of proposed scheme.
g) Marketing of radio and tape recorder products from Eastern Europe.
h) Any other business.

(*b*) administering funds or property;
(*c*) carrying out the aims of the larger group – business and commerce, education, charitable activities, acting as pressure groups;
(*d*) appointing and dismissing employees;
(*e*) maintaining adequate records;
(*f*) carrying out the requirements of the law – paying taxes, VAT, rates, observing factory regulations, office regulations, health and safety regulations.

As their business will be more detailed, the agenda should reflect this difference (see Example 33).

The minutes of meetings

At many meetings those present will make notes of what has been said and done. The more there are that do this the greater is the likelihood that conflicting accounts will be made. To avoid this conflict one person is responsible for producing an official record of what took place at a meeting. The person is usually the secretary, although sometimes there is a minute secretary whose sole function is to produce a record of the meeting.

The secretary is not expected to make a verbatim report because much may be said that is irrelevant or trivial.

What kind of information should be recorded? The following represents a basic minimum.

(*a*) Date and place of meeting.
(*b*) The fact that those present have agreed to the minutes of the preceding meeting as representing a true record.
(*c*) Who was present? The name of the Chairman is usually recorded. The number present is stated.
(*d*) All motions of discussion that have been formally presented. The names of those proposing and seconding are given. When the motion has been put to the vote a record of the voting is made. Sometimes a summary of the arguments for and against a motion may be included although this is less important than the decision reached.
(*e*) The names of all people appointed to hold office or to be members of any committee. The names of those proposing and seconding should be given and the voting figures where a vote is taken.
(*f*) Reports. A report may be summarised or printed in full and given as an appendix. If the former the name of the person making the report should be stated. If the latter, there should be a minute to the effect that the report was made. When the accounts are presented these are usually offered as an appendix.
(*g*) Discussion which does not lead to formal motions should be summarised to record the essential points. The secretary will use

her judgement when deciding whether to include the names of those making particular points.

(*h*) Correspondence that is brought before a meeting should be referred to briefly. Any relevant discussion or decisions relating to it should be given.

The following (Examples 34 and 35) are examples of the Minutes of Meetings.

ANNUAL GENERAL MEETING

Example 34

Note to Example 34

These Minutes are a formal record of the meeting and are a statement of business transacted. The Chairman's Report and the Statement of

Minutes of the 10th Annual General Meeting of the Newtown Electronics Company Ltd., held on 24th May, 1980, at the Newtown Civic Hall, in the Queen's Room.

1. The meeting was opened at 5.30 p.m. by the Chairman, Major L. Sparkes.

2. Minutes.

   The minutes of the 9th Annual General Meeting, held on 23rd May, 1979, having been previously circulated, were confirmed by the meeting.

3. Business arising.

   Col. the Hon. Sir Stafford Staples, K.B.E.

   The Chairman reported that he had written to Col. The Hon. Sir Stafford Staples, K.B.E., a former President of the Company, to congratulate him on his appointment as Lord Lieutenant of the County of Hopeshire. Sir Stafford's letter of reply was read out.

4. Chairman's Report.

   The Chairman presented his report on the progress of the Company for the year ending 31st March, 1980. He drew particular attention to the expansion of the Company's activities at Newtown and to the Board's decision to build and open premises at Portville, Bordertown and Marshington. This had had a favourable effect on the Company's finances and the resulting final dividend. After some discussion the Report was adopted. (See Appendix A.)

5. Presentation of the Audited Accounts and Balance Sheet.

Mr. Shilling, the Company's Chief Accountant, in presenting the Annual Accounts, referred to the printed statement which members had received. He went through them, drawing attention to items he felt members would wish to be explained. He supported the Chairman in his remarks concerning the progress made but was most concerned at the effect that the Government's taxation of companies would have in the future. He expressed his appreciation of the work done by the Company's auditors.

After Mr. Shilling had dealt with the questions of those present, the meeting adopted the statement of accounts. (See Appendix B.)

6. Appointment of Officers and other members of the Board.

The Secretary referred to the arrangements that had been made for the appointment of officers and members of the Board and announced the results.

a) The Officers: The Board has re-nominated the Chairman and Vice-Chairman to serve another year. There had been no other nominations. He asked the meeting to give its approval. This was given unanimously.

b) The Board: The Chairman announced that one-third of the Board were due to retire this year. All, except Sir Stanley Mustang and Dr. Alan Hopeful, had indicated their willingness to serve another three years. These had been re-nominated. He called upon the Secretary to announce the results of the election.

These were:

Adam, J. C.	780	Everite, F. M.	777
Ball, K. M.	767	Frieston, S. H. V.	648
Beaming, Miss A. L.	791	Grimely, Mrs. V. W.	736
Brander, Sir L.	800	Hagler, The Hon. F. M.	750
Cuter, Ms. S. T.	650	Jexon, P. P.	817
Dorlass, Dr. A. P.	770	The Lord Kipple	790
Eastwell, Sir S. S.	823	Sandieford, L. V.	792

All except Ms. S. T. Cuter and S. H. V. Frieston were declared elected to the Board.

The Secretary proposed a vote of thanks to Sir Stanley Mustang and Dr. Alan Hopeful for their most helpful services as members of the Board since the Company's formation. This was seconded by the Vice-Chairman and approved by the meeting.

7. Appointment of Auditors.

Mr. Shilling, the Chief Accountant, proposed that Messrs. Bunting and Finch be re-appointed as Auditors for the ensuing year. This was seconded by Mr. S. Smith. The meeting approved.

There being no other formal business on the Agenda, the meeting was declared closed at 7.00 p.m.

Accounts are very briefly referred to, the full report and statement being included as Appendices, which were presented but are not printed in this book.

GENERAL MEETINGS

Example 35

Minutes of the General Meeting of the Hopeshire County Preservation Society held on Friday, July 20th, 1980, at 7.30 p.m. at Oldchurch Community Centre.

1. Chairman. Mr. Lawrence Towneley, in the chair, opened the meeting at 7.30 p.m.

2. Minutes.
The Minutes of the General Meeting held on Friday, January 19th, were confirmed by the meeting, and signed by the Chairman.

3. Business arising.
a) Proposed Oldchurch By-pass. The Secretary stated that he had written to the County Council Chairman to express the Society's concern for the effect that the new by-pass would have on the bird population of the area. The County Council Chairman had replied that the letter was being presented to the County Highways Committee at its next meeting on July 31st, 1980.
b) Sandy Marsh Scheme. The Secretary had written to the secretary of Hopeshire Naturalist Trust about the Sandy Marsh scheme. He welcomed the Society's approach and promised to keep the secretary informed of proposed future developments.

4. Correspondence.
The Secretary read a letter he had received from the Chairman of the Hopeshire County Council Planning Committee concerning proposals for the development of the town centre of Portville. It was suggested that the Society nominate a representative to serve on a committee being appointed to examine this. The meeting agreed to the Secretary's proposal that the Chairman's name be sent to the County. The meeting instructed the Secretary to make it clear that this nomination did not imply approval of any plans that might be announced.

5. Chairman's Report.
In his report the Chairman outlined the various activities that the Committee had been following. These included various projects on the Society's property and participation in activities organised by various local communities.

6. Financial Statement for the first quarter.

The Treasurer presented his statement, a copy of which is given as an appendix to the Minutes. He was very pleased to note that the membership secretary's activities were resulting in a larger return from subscriptions at this time of the year.

7. Marina at Seabridge: effects on Hopeshire Marshes.

The Secretary gave an account of Seabridge District Council's proposals to build a marina at Seabridge. These had been circulated to interested bodies. It was intended to have an open meeting at Seabridge early in September. The Committee had invited Dr. Julian Strong to prepare a memorandum on the effects this would have on Hopeshire Marshes. His preliminary findings give cause for concern. An animated discussion followed.

It was agreed that the Secretary write to Seabridge District Council to express concern, especially at the destruction of the medieval harbour. The meeting also requested the Secretary to urge all members to attend the September meeting or write to Seabridge Council.

8. County Survey of Butterflies.

The Chairman introduced the Committee's proposal to carry out a county survey of butterflies in 1981. A small sub-committee of three enthusiasts was appointed to prepare details of this. They would be reporting at the next general meeting. The general enthusiasm was reflected in the many favourable comments expressed and questions asked by the members. The meeting endorsed the committee's appointment of the sub-committee and agreed to the survey being made.

9. Other Business.

The Chairman reported that he had not received notices of other business.

10. Date and place of next meeting.

This was fixed for Friday, October 26th, 1980, at 7.30 p.m. to be held at Seabridge Unicorn Hall.

Note to Example 35

Although the Hopeshire County Preservation Society is registered as a limited company, it is also a charity and a body that hopes to influence others. Its general meetings provide the opportunity to gather together interested people and its agenda reflects its range of interests. It should be noted, however, that they are Minutes, a summarised report of what was done and decided. They are not intended to be a verbatim report.

Summary of correspondence

In many situations an item or transaction may be spread over a period of time and involve numerous pieces of correspondence. On occasions the matters being dealt with will involve communication with others. It may be helpful if the contents of all the correspondence can be summarised on one sheet so that the reader can readily grasp the situation.

Consider the letter shown in Example 36.

Example 36

4 Princes Rise,
Newtown,
Hopeshire.

May 5th, 1980

The Manager,
Newtown Housing Committee,
Newtown.

Dear Sir,

I have lived in this house for the past thirty years and in this time have had very few occasions to write about repairs.

During the past few weeks I have noticed that the upstairs ceiling is wet. It is probable that there are loose tiles on the roof. Would you send someone to look at this?

The paint on the outside of the house is also peeling. We have not had any external decorating for the past four years. Can you tell me when it will be done?

Yours faithfully,

A. Tenant. (Mrs.)

This letter is passed to the Area Maintenance Officer. He has a file relating to 4 Princes Rise. He places the letter in it and on a contents sheet fills in briefly what the letter is about (see Example 37).

In summary notes details are entered that are useful to the Maintenance Section.

The Area Maintenance Officer's reply is shown in Example 38.

Example 37

NEWTOWN DISTRICT COUNCIL. HOUSING MAINTENANCE.

Mrs. A. Tenant - 4 Princes Rise.

CONTENTS OF FILE.

5.5.80. A. Tenant to Housing Manager

i) wet upstairs ceiling - loose tiles on roof.
ii) outside paint peeling - not decorated for 4 yrs.

Example 38

Newtown District Council

North Area Maintenance Office.
North Way,
Newtown.

May 7th, 1980

Mrs A. Tenant,
4 Princes Rise,
Newtown.

Dear Mrs. Tenant,

Repairs - 4 Princes Rise.

Thank you for your letter of May 5th, 1980, which has been passed to me.

I have asked our roof maintenance officer to call to see you. He ought to be along early next week.

I am sorry about the exterior condition. This decoration is let out to contract. Your area is down to be started in September - but this will depend on the weather. I shall let you know when we can start.

Yours sincerely,
John Plumber.
Area Maintenance Officer.

Mr. Plumber places his copy in the file and enters the second item on the contents sheet (Example 39).

Example 39

```
7/5/80. A.M.O. to A. Tenant.
 i) sending roof maintenance officer - following week.
ii) informed that area due for repainting in September, subject to
    weather.
```

The roof maintenance officer called and confirmed that there was a loose tile. A workman replaced it. A week later there was a heavy storm and the ceiling was wet again – this time in another area. She wrote the following letter (Example 40.

Example 40

```
                                        4 Princes Rise,
                                        Newtown,
                                        Hopeshire.

                                        May 30th, 1980.

North Area Maintenance Office,
North Way,
Newtown.


Dear Sir,

                    House Repairs - 4 Princes Rise.

     I wrote to you on May 5th. Following your reply on May 7th,
the roof officer called on Thursday, May 10th, and said he would
send someone to repair the roof.  A week later the roofmen came
and fixed the loose tiles.
     On Monday this week we had that heavy rainstorm.  Last night I
went into the upstairs room and noticed that it was wet again - but
this time in the opposite corner.
     Could you please do something about it?

                         Yours faithfully,
                                   A. Tenant. (Mrs.)
```

The contents sheet in the file for 4 Princes Rise will have the following details added (Example 41).

Example 41

```
30/5/80. A. Tenant to A.M.O.
 i) acknowledged work done by roof repairs.
ii) following heavy rainstorm 28/5/80 - another ceiling leak.
```

On 4th June, the roof inspector calls and states that he cannot find anything wrong. On June 5th and June 6th there is very heavy rain and water pours from the ceiling on to the carpet and armchair.

Mrs. A. Tenant writes again (Example 42).

Example 42

4 Princes Rise,
Newtown,
Hopeshire.

June 7th, 1980

North Area Maintenance Officer,
North Way,
Newtown.

Dear Sir,

Roof Leak - 4 Princes Rise.

In spite of my letter of May 30th, nothing has been done. The roof inspector said he could find nothing wrong. As you know, we have had heavy rain on June 5th and 6th. The water is now pouring from the ceiling.

The carpet, which I only bought 3 months ago, has been saturated and is now stained. The water has also run on to an armchair and has stained it.

I am not satisfied and I am going to take this further.

Yours faithfully,
A. Tenant. (Mrs.)

Mrs. Tenant does so. She writes to her M.P. and he writes to the Chief Executive Officer of Newtown District Council demanding compensation for the damage done to the carpet and chair as well as action about the roof.

The Executive Officer asks the Housing Manager for a report and a summary of the letters that have been sent. This summary consists of the entries that have been made on the contents sheet and reads as follows (Example 43):

Example 43

```
Summary of correspondence between Mrs. A. Tenant and Housing
Department concerning repairs to 4 Princes Rise, Newtown.

5/5/80. A. Tenant to Housing Manager.
         i) wet upstairs ceiling - loose tiles on roof,
        ii) outside paint peeling - not decorated for 4 years.

7/5/80. Area Maintenance Officer to A. Tenant.
         i) sending roof maintenance officer - following week,
        ii) informed that area due for painting in Sept., subject
            to weather.

30/5/80. A. Tenant to A.M.O.
         i) acknowledged work done by roof repairers,
        ii) following heavy rainstorm 28/5/80 - another leak.

7/6/80. A. Tenant to A.M.O.
          i) complaint of no action,
         ii) further rain on 5/6 and 6/6 - water pouring
             through ceiling,
        iii) damage to carpet and armchair,
         iv) promises to take matter further.
```

It is important that in a summary of correspondence the following information is given for each letter:

1. name of sender;
2. name of person to whom sent;
3. date of letter;
4. a brief statement, expressed clearly, of each subject mentioned.

Summary in note-form

As well as correspondence it may also be necessary to summarise memoranda, reports, statements, newspaper articles. This involves reading the passage, grasping its meaning and deciding what is required for reproduction or summary. The writer is next concerned with presentation. She will have to decide if any of the material needs rearranging and what is to be its layout – division into sections or sub-sections, the provision of suitable headings or sub-headings and the discreet use of underlining or variation in the type face.

The following passage illustrates use of note-form summary. Read this passage carefully.

Education for young people after sixteen

John Smith has reached the age of sixteen. As the term or session moves towards its end he is confronted first by the prospect of 'O' Levels or C.S.E.s, and, after that, by the promised land of the future, to leave school and start work. The alternative is to continue his education.

What education is open to him and all the other sixteen-year-olds? It is most likely that, during the fifth year, their headteachers will have suggested the sixth form. The bright ones who obtain a reasonable number of good 'O' Level passes will opt for academic courses leading to university. They will study for 'A' Levels in three subjects, all satisfying entrance demands to degree courses.

The not-so-bright students with few 'O' Level passes will be encouraged to re-take failed subjects and try perhaps one 'A' Level. The careers staff will turn the attention of these students to work in industry and commerce. The weakest ones will regard the extra year as an opportunity to obtain one or two 'O' Level passes in basic subjects.

Our fifth formers will not only have the advice and guidance of school staff. They will have the chance to get help from the local Careers Advisory Service for school leavers. Most of them will have friends who have left school, some to continue their education. These two groups will, between them, cause many to turn their attention to a college of further education or to a technical college where the aim is to help prepare students for particular types of employment. As the leavers study the various prospectuses they will discover an interesting range of courses – motor vehicle maintenance, printing, photography, journalism, medical and dental technicians, business studies, nursing cadets, child care, catering, hairdressing, retail trading and computer studies, to name but a few. These courses offer training at various levels. The work done will be a mixture of the practical and the relevant theoretical. At the end of the courses they will take and obtain the qualifications for which they have been studying.

From their contacts the brighter children learn that these colleges also provide routes of study to colleges of higher education, colleges of technology, polytechnics and even universities. The range of courses will seem to have a wider scope and the students at school will come to believe that they have a better chance of success at one of these colleges.

Not only do the colleges of further education and technical colleges offer more varied and attractive courses; the students realise that the approach is different. They will be treated as adults; they will not be surrounded by lots of younger children. There appear to be fewer rules – they can wear what they like, they are not shepherded about the premises and nobody stops them smoking. The students around them are mostly of their own age, but some are older. Other students will tell them of happy relationships with their tutors. If to this is added the fact that most colleges offer a wider range of 'O' and 'A' Levels than is available at school it is not surprising that many sixteen-year-olds are tempted in this direction with the result that school sixth forms may become smaller than they should be. This creates problems in the use of staff, physical and financial resources and in deciding the curriculum to be followed.

These problems have led to further experiments – the sixth form college and what are called 'tertiary' colleges. Some will now be considered, and, following this, the opportunities in further education for those still at work.

The following (Example 44a) are **first** notes based on the passage.

Example 44a

Para. 1 *Introductory.* Suggest options for a sixteen-year-old:
(*a*) Work; or (*b*) Continued education.

Para. 2 *Poses main topic of passage.* 'What education is open to the sixteen-year-old?'
School advice – sixth Form.
Bright ones: Academic. Three 'A' Levels – leads to University.
Medium: a few 'O' Levels. Chance to re-take failed subjects and one 'A' Level. Their course leads to industry and commerce.
Weak: Gives further time to try for a couple of basic 'O' Levels.

Para. 3 *Other advice.* From: (*a*) Careers; (*b*) former pupils.
They suggest (i) College of Further Education, or
(ii) Technical College
which: offer a wide range of vocational courses at varying levels;
are practical and theoretical;
lead to vocational qualifications.

Para. 4 *Bright students.* F.E. Colleges lead to:
College of Higher Education;
College of Advanced Technology;
Polytechnics – University.
A wider range of courses – prospects of better success.

Para. 5 *College of Further Education.* Approach different:
adult – no younger children;
fewer rules;
students same age (a few older);
happy tutor/student relationships.
They also offer 'O' and 'A' Levels – a much wider range.
All this tempts sixteen-year-olds from the sixth form.
Result: smaller sixth forms;
problems:
(*a*) staff size;
(*b*) limit to resources, finances
(*c*) effect on curriculum.

Para. 6 (*i*) *Further experiments:* sixth form colleges; Tertiary colleges.
(*ii*) *Further education* available for younger school leavers.

Notes to Example 44a

The task is to construct a summary in note-form with an effective layout. A study of the above raises these questions:

(*a*) Is paragraph 1 necessary in the summary?

(*b*) What headings would be helpful?

(i) Sixth Form opportunities.

(ii) College of further education technical college.

The following (Example 44b) is offered as a summary in note-form of the passage.

Example 44b Education for Young People After Sixteen.

What educational opportunities are there for young people at sixteen?

1. The Sixth Form at School.
   The sixteen-year-old is advised by school staff to go into the sixth form.
   The bright ones – to do academic courses of 3 'A' Levels – leads to University.
   Medium ability – have a few 'O' Levels: chance to re-take failed subjects plus 1 'A' Level – the aim is commerce and industry.
   Weak scholars – gives further time to try to obtain a couple of basic 'O' Levels.
2. A College of Further Education or Technical College.
   The sixteen-year-old also receives advice from: the Careers Service; and former pupils of his or her school. They recommend the college of further education or a technical college which offer:
   (*a*) a wide range of vocational courses;
   (*b*) courses at various levels;
   (*c*) courses which are both practical and theoretical.
   For the brighter student there is a wider range of courses which
   1. offer better prospects of success;
   2. lead to higher level colleges and institutions.
3. The College of Further Education Attracts Potential Sixth Form Students.
   (*a*) The college approach is different:
   – adult;
   – fewer rules;
   – students same age – some older;
   – happy tutor/student relationships.
   (*b*) The college also offers 'O' and 'A' Level courses in a wider range of subjects.
   (*c*) The result is the smaller sixth form with its detrimental effect on:
   (i) the ratio of staff in a school;
   (ii) the amount of finance and resources available;

(iii) the school curriculum.
(*d*) These problems have led to new experiments.
4. The Sixth Form College.
5. The Tertiary College.

The passage at greater length will expand on each of these. It will then examine the provision for the continued education of the school leaver at work.

The synopsis, digest and abstract

These three different forms of extended summary can be produced by students capable of writing either a précis (with which 'O' Level candidates in English Language should be familiar) or a note-form summary (described above).

SYNOPSIS

A synopsis is a short detailed summary, larger than the average table of contents, of what is to be found in a book, or part of a book. The following is a synopsis by the author of the second part of this work.

'In Part 2 of this work I have examined the various types of written communication in use in most organisations. In the first section I have examined those types of communication used internally – the memo, the notice and the longer memorandum. The basic feature of each type is described in detail and followed by suitable examples. The study has then moved from within the system to the world beyond the organisation. The commonest form is the letter, of which there are many types. These have been described and followed by examples. The other widely used forms are the telegram and Telex message, both of which are described and illustrated. The third section deals extensively with the composition and format of the written report, in both letter and memorandum form.'

DIGEST

The digest is a condensed form of a written or printed work. The art of producing a digest lies in deciding what has to be left out. What is the most essential part of a novel? In most cases one would say, 'the story which shows the working out of the author's plot'. The aim of the writer of the digest would therefore be to rewrite the main plot using the author's own language. Other elements can be omitted – or reduced. Thus, the digest writer could remove passages of descriptive writing or eliminate those containing the narrator's observations or commentary.

ABSTRACT

Many technical publications contain some information not needed by their readers. The writer of an abstract should select and then summarise the sections that are required.

Charts and diagrams

Note-form summary helps a reader to understand more quickly the contents of a passage of writing. In this section other ways of achieving this will be studied.

Some college students conducted an enquiry into how students used the different mass media. One student presented his information as follows.

There are 500 students in this college of whom 275 are men. 250 men and 200 women have a television set at home. Of them 200 men and 160 women have colour sets. 100 men and 60 women watch BBC 2. 225 men and 180 women watch ITV. 200 men and 180 women watch BBC 1. All the students have some kind of radio set. 50 men and 25 women listen to Radio 3. 225 men and 225 women listen to both Radio 1 and Radio 2. 200 men and 225 women listen to Radio 4. 150 men and 200 women listen to other radio stations. 75 men and 50 women say they never read a newspaper. 50 men and 30 women only read papers on Sunday. 100 men read 'The Sun', 100 men read the 'Daily Mail', 75 men read the 'Guardian' and 120 men read the 'Daily Telegraph'. The numbers of women reading these papers are 80, 120, 90 and 150 respectively. On Sunday, 80 men and 60 women read the 'Observer', 75 men and 75 women the 'Sunday Telegraph', 120 men and 150 women the 'Sunday Mirror', 150 men and 180 women the 'News of the World', and 130 men and 150 women the 'People'.

This student's presentation makes the information difficult to follow and understand. It can be presented differently.

NEWMINSTER COLLEGE
Use of the media by the students
275 men : 275 women

A. *TELEVISION*

	Men	Women
1. Number with set at home	250	200
2. Number who watch:		
BBC 1	200	180
BBC 2	100	80
ITV	225	180

B. *RADIO*

	Men	Women
1. Number with set	275	275
2. Number who listen to:		
Radio 1	225	225
Radio 2	225	225
Radio 3	50	25
Radio 4	200	225
Other stations	150	200

C. *NEWSPAPERS*

	Men	Women
1. Number who read daily papers:		
Daily Mail	100	120
Daily Telegraph	120	150
Guardian	75	90
Sun	100	80
2. Number who read Sunday papers:		
News of the World	150	180
Observer	80	60
People	130	150
Sunday Mirror	120	150
Sunday Telegraph	75	75
3. Number who do not read any paper	75	50

This information has been presented in tabular form which makes it easily followed. In this form inferences may be made or conclusions reached more easily from the figures.

In the next example the information has been presented in graphical form (Fig. 1). It shows the monthly sales of cars by one company over a period of two years, 1978 and 1979. The different kind of line indicates the year. The advantage of the graph is that it enables the company to compare sales performances for any month in each of the two years.

The type of diagram shown in Fig. 1 is useful for measuring quantities in relation to the movement of time. The variation in quantities in relation to other things may also be expressed by this type of diagram. For instance, one can indicate the number of boys of varying heights in a class and comparison can be made with the number of girls of varying heights in the same class. These variations may also be expressed by symbolic pictures (Fig. 2).

Information concerning proportions and percentages may also be presented as a diagram or chart, with the use of areas to convey the information (Fig. 3).

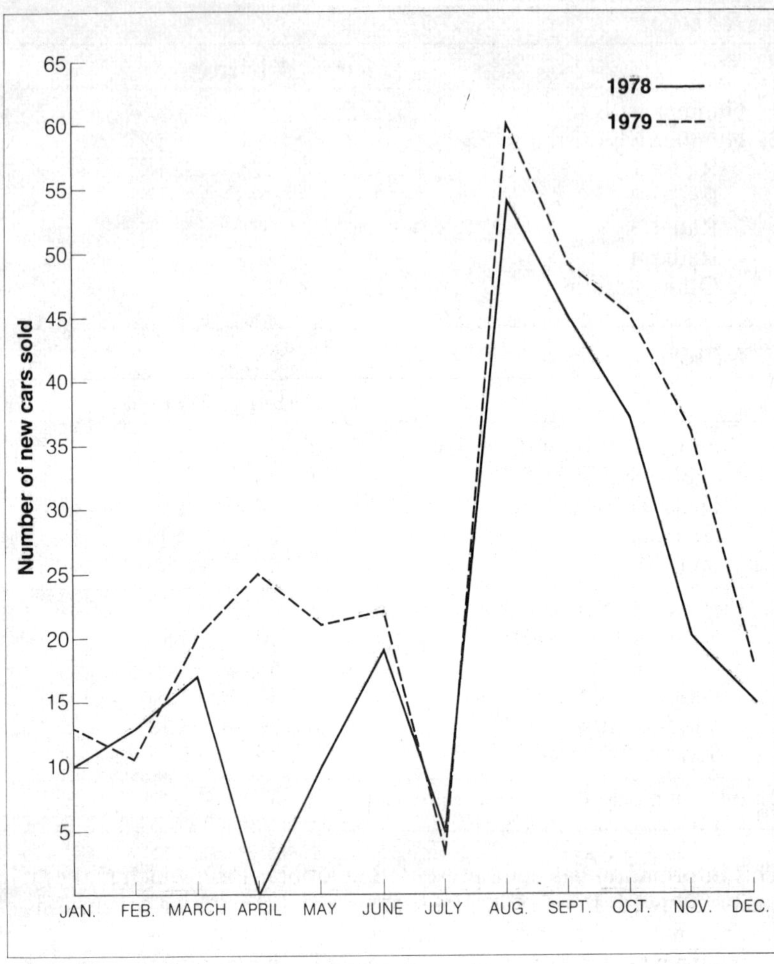
1978
1979
Number of new cars sold
65
60
55
50
45
40
35
30
25
20
15
10
5
JAN.
FEB.
MARCH
APRIL
MAY
JUNE
JULY
AUG.
SEPT.
OCT.
NOV.
DEC.

Fig. 1

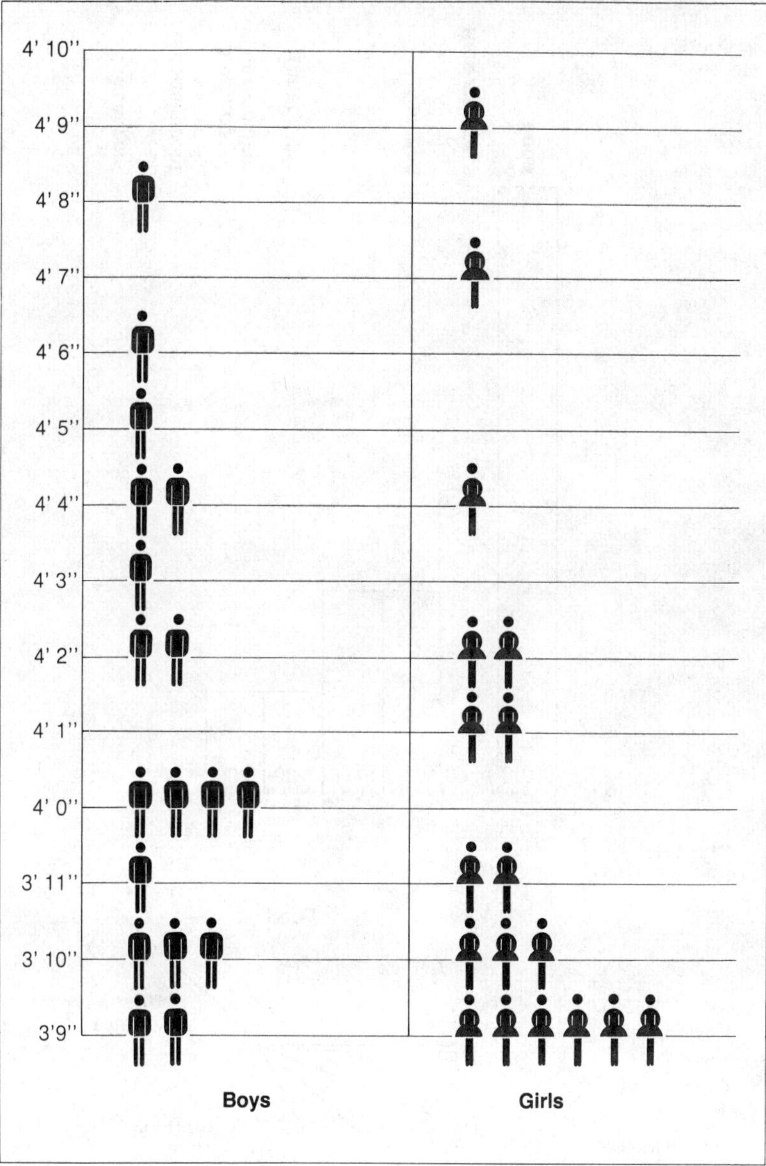

Fig. 2

Forms and questionnaires

These are two time-saving methods of communication for those seeking information from others but their design must enable them to be readily understood and easily completed.

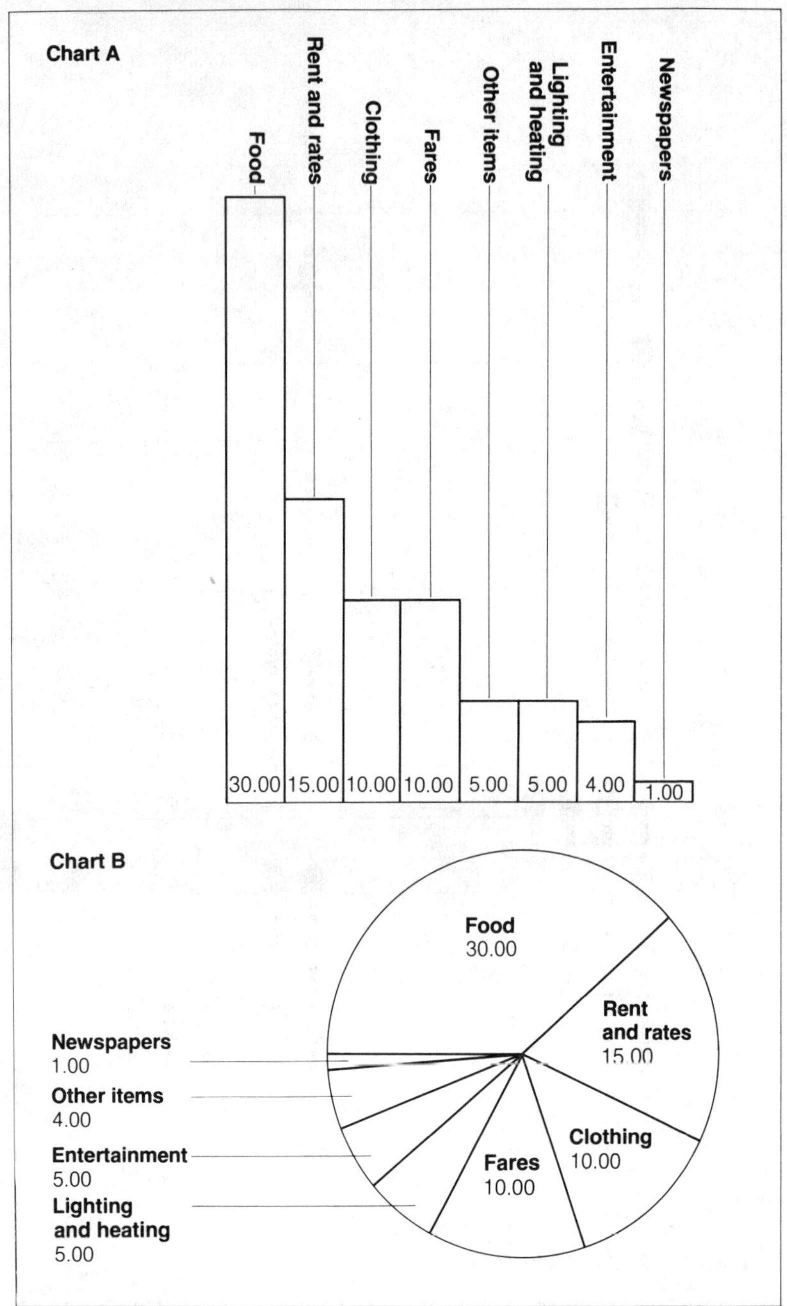

Fig. 3 Chart A shows a breakdown of expenditure of a weekly wage of £80. Chart B is another way of showing the same information.

The **form** seeks information that enables the person sending it out to take action or make a decision.

The following are examples of forms:

1. Form of application for a passport. From the information the Passport Office:
   (*a*) decides if the applicant is entitled to a passport or not;
   (*b*) prepares the passport.
2. Form of application for employment. When completed it enables the prospective employer:
   (*a*) to decide if the candidate meets the requirements to enable him/her to be considered;
   (*b*) to transfer to the organisation's records all relevant information.
3. An order form enables a supplier:
   (*a*) to prepare for despatch goods required by the purchaser;
   (*b*) to prepare any documents relevant to the transaction (e.g. invoices, address labels).

The **questionnaire** seeks more general information. It is frequently used in surveys for statistical purposes or to enable companies to discover, for instance, how successful are their advertising methods or how satisfactory are their products.

The following are examples:

(*a*) The National Census form. Its purpose is to provide the Government with information about people to enable it to make various statistical summaries. (N.B. There is a tendency to use the word 'form' instead of questionnaire.)
(*b*) Many suppliers issue a card to their customers, for completion and return, requesting information about how they heard of the firm's products.
(*c*) Some manufacturers send to purchasers questionnaires about performance.

COMPILING FORMS

The following points should be considered when compiling forms:
What information is required?
Are you being *too* inquisitive?
Are the questions clear?
Are the instructions about recording answers easy to follow?
Has enough space been given to enable information to be written down?
Is the form's layout easy to follow?
Is the address to which the form is to be sent clearly stated?

COMPILING QUESTIONNAIRES

What information is wanted?

Are the questions relevant to the information being sought?
Do you want answers of the Yes/No/Don't Know types? If so, is this indicated in the question?
Do you want descriptive or narrative answers? Do the questions make it clear what you want to know?
Has enough room been given for replies?
Do you need the name and address of those completing the questionnaire?
Have you indicated why you want the questionnaire completed?

Example 45 is a form of application for employment.

Example 45 (see pages 71–73)

Notes to Example 45

1. The form should provide the company's name and address.
2. This is a general application form. The nature of the post should be entered by the company, or by the applicant.
3. Information required.
   (*a*) Basic personal information. Many forms also include marital status, nationality and national insurance details. Before including them the person preparing the form should ask if the extra information is necessary from all applicants or from the successful applicant only.
   (*b*) Education. For what posts is the form intended? If a high level of education is expected (e.g. a degree or higher professional qualifications) a form demanding more detailed information than is required for the average employee should be designed. School – generally it is unnecessary to ask for information earlier than the age of fourteen. Questions should recognise that education may be private as well as state-controlled. Examinations. Is it necessary to ask a candidate to list his/her failures as well as successes?
   (*c*) Employment. Information should enable an interviewer to assess the candidate's suitability. Any further information for administrative and record purposes may be obtained from the successful candidate later.
   (*d*) References. If one must be a character reference this should be made clear.
   (*e*) Further Information. This section should be so worded that the candidate knows what is expected.
4. Instructions. On this form instructions concerning name of person to receive the application and the final date are left to the end. The date has to be typed in.
5. Before the form is printed ensure that it contains the essential details.

NEWTOWN ELECTRONICS COMPANY LIMITED

Head Office: 1 Faraday Lane, Newtown, Hopeshire

FORM OF APPLICATION FOR SHORTHAND TYPIST.

1. Surname 2. Mr/Miss/Mrs.
3. Forenames
4. Date of Birth 5. Age
6. Address

7. Telephone Number

Details of Education.

8. Schools attended since the age of 14.

(To be given in chronological order.)

	Name of School.	From.	To.
a			
b			
c			

9. Further and Higher Education.

	Name of College or Institute.	Years.
a		
b		

10. Examinations Passed.

(a) C.S.E. and G.C.E.

Subject. C.S.E./G.C.E. Level. Grade.	Subject. C.S.E./G.C.E. Level. Grade.
i	v
ii	vi
iii	vii
iv	viii

(b) Other examining bodies.

	Name of body.	Exam. taken.	Subjects.	Result.
i				
ii				
iii				

Details of Employment.

11. Present Employment.

Name of employer.

Address.

Employer's business.

Nature of applicant's work. Present Salary.

Time applicant has worked for this employer. From. To.

(Give exact details.)

12. Previous Employers

Please give details of all previous employments.

	Name and Address.	Types of work done.	Time in employment. From.	To.
i				
ii				
iii				
iv				
v				

13. References.

Please give details of two persons to whom reference may be made concerning your suitability for this post, one of whom should be your present employer.

1) Name.
   Address.
   Status.
2) Name.
   Address.
   Status.

Do you wish us to write to your present employer before an interview has been held or after?

BEFORE/AFTER. Please delete as appropriate.

14. The candidate may use this space to give further information that he/she considers relevant to this application. It may also be used to write a letter of application for the post.

Signature of candidate.
Date.

When completed this form should be sent to reach Mrs. A. Watkinson, Personnel Officer, at Head Office, not later than ....

Example 46 is an order form for goods from a mail order catalogue.

Example 46 (see page 74)

Notes to Example 46

1. Name and address of suppliers to be set out clearly.
2. The order.
   The company uses the catalogue number for its stock records. The description enables a check to be made should the customer have quoted the wrong number.
   Number. Price. Total cost. These will aid the preparation of the invoice and the despatch note.
   Totals and postage. It must be made clear that the customer is to complete these.

To: NEWTOWN UNIVERSAL STORES LTD.
15-17 Princetown Way, Newtown, Hopeshire.

Will you please send the following goods described in your Summer Catalogue for 1980?

Catalogue number	Description	Number required	Price	Total cost

Name:

Total.

Plus postage.
(See page 3 of catalogue.)

Total amount.

Method of payment.

1. CASH. I enclose cheque no. .... for £.............
   OR
2. CREDIT CARD. I wish to pay for the above goods by credit card, details of which are:
   BARCLAYCARD/ACCESS/AMERICAN EXPRESS. (Delete as necessary.)

NUMBER | | | | | | | | | | | | | |

SIGNATURE........................

DATE.............................

3. CREDIT TERMS. I wish to pay in accordance with the terms in your catalogue. I am over 18. Signature............................
   Date.................................

Further information required – name and address of customer and method of payment. The order form should set out the methods of payment permitted. The customer's signature is formally required if she wishes to pay by credit card or have credit facilities from the company.

Example 47 is a questionnaire about goods purchased.

Example 47

WONDER DOMESTIC MACHINES.

Dear Customer,

Congratulations on acquiring your new Wonder Domestic Blender Mixer 1980 Model.

We are sure that you will have many years of valuable use from it and that your family and friends will enjoy the exciting new dishes that you will be offering them.

We should be very pleased if you would complete the following questionnaire which will help us in our future planning. When you have completed it, all you have to do is to fold it as indicated and post it. No stamp is needed.

Questionnaire.

1. How did you hear about Wonder Domestic Blender Mixer?

- by television ☐
- by advertisement in i) a newspaper. ☐
  give name..............................
  ii) a weekly magazine. ☐
  give name..............................
- through our leaflet campaign in your area ☐
- from a friend ☐
- by recommendation from a dealer ☐
- in any other way ☐
  (Give brief details.)

2. Have you ever used a Blender/Mixer before? YES/NO
   If so, please give make.......................................
3. Have you ever used any Wonder Domestic Products before?
   YES/NO. If so, name product...................................
4. Would you like to know the ways in which your Wonder Domestic Blender Mixer can make your life more exciting? YES/NO
   If the answer is Yes, may we send you our new 1980 Recipe Leaflet? YES/NO

   We will also send you details of the new 1980 WONDER DOMESTIC RECIPES of BRITAIN.

If the answer to question 4 was YES, please give -
your name................................
your address.............................
....

Notes to Example 47

1. The introductory section has been written to encourage the purchaser of this article to complete the questionnaire.
2. Question 1. These questions enable the company to assess the success of its own advertising campaign.
3. Question 2. This enables the company to assess its effectiveness over competitors.
4. Question 3. This answers the question, 'Does our reputation enable us to sell goods?'
5. Question 4. This has been designed to enable the purchaser to send her name and address. She will get a free leaflet and the company might be able to sell her a book. In any case, it can send details of new products.

A company is considering changing its system of working hours and decides to ask its staff for information.

Example 48

NEWTOWN ELECTRONICS LIMITED

To: All employees of the company.
From: The General Manager.
Date: December 31st, 1980.

Re-examination of Hours of Employment.

Following suggestions made to the Personnel Officer and myself, the management are considering a change in the Company's hours of employment. It will be most helpful if you would complete and return this questionnaire to me as soon as possible. It is not necessary to sign your name at the end.

1. How do you travel to work? - by train
   - by bus
   - by taxi
   - by private car or motor cycle
   - by cycle
   - on foot

   Please tick the method used.
2. If you travel by train give the time
   (a) when you leave in the morning........................
   (b) when you arrive at Newtown Station...................
   (c) when the train before yours arrives..................
   (d) when the train after yours arrives...................

3. If you travel by bus state
   (a) how long the journey takes.............................
   (b) how frequent are the buses
       on your route...
4. If you travel by any other method than bus or train are there any special traffic problems that affect the time of your arrival at work?..
   If so, list them briefly...
   ....
5. Would it help if you were able to start work a) earlier or b) later? Please indicate which......................................
6. Would it help if you were to finish work a) earlier or b) later? Please indicate which......................................
7. Would you take advantage of a scheme to enable you
   (a) to take your children to school? YES/NO
   (b) to be at home for your children at the end of school? YES/NO
   If you had to choose between (a) or (b) which would you prefer? ......
8. Would you like to do your shopping before coming to work? YES/NO
9. Would you like to be able to leave earlier to do your shopping? YES/NO
   If so, would you be willing to start work earlier at some other time? YES/NO
10. Have you any problem that would be made easier by a variation in working hours? YES/NO
    If so, it would help if you would state what the problem is
    ....
11. If you have any comments to make about the present system of working hours, or if you can suggest any possible changes, will you please write them below?
    ....
    ....

COMPLETING FORMS AND QUESTIONNAIRES

1. Before any questions are answered the form or questionnaire must be read carefully. Any supplementary explanatory notes must also be read.
2. If a question asks for information that information alone should be given.
3. Similarly a question inviting the answer 'Yes' or 'No' requires no further details.
4. From the above it follows that lengthier answers should be given only when the question demands it.

5. Although forms should be designed so that plenty of room exists for the answers, this is not always so. Clumsy alterations to an answer may make it difficult to understand what has been written. People completing forms would be well advised to use pencil first or, even better, to draft out the answers on a separate sheet of paper.

ly, put an enc
vileges etc.) [F
tion (æbəlíʃə
g ‖ (esp. hi
lavery abolitio
L. abolitio (a

Assignments in communication

Part 3

Each of the assignments which follow is based on a working situation in which the student might find herself involved. Sometimes she is asked to imagine herself filling different roles. In the classroom these roles could be allocated to different students. The material presented here will help the student to make use of the information given in the earlier parts of this book.

Assignment No. 1

You work for Messrs. Raven & Swallow, booksellers, of 6 North Street, Newtown, Hopeshire. On Saturday, customers ordered the books which are listed below. They were not in stock and have now to be ordered.

1. Produce separate lists for each publisher, with the books arranged in alphabetical order of the authors' names. If more than one book by an author is given, arrange his books in alphabetical order of the titles. If the title starts with 'A' or 'The' these words come first.
2. Select the list for Longman. Prepare a letter to be sent to this firm to order the books. The address may be found in the Cambridge section of the telephone directory or obtained by enquiry at any public library.
3. When the order is dealt with, the publisher will:
   (*a*) send the books, if available; or
   (*b*) inform you that a book is being reprinted or rebound and that it will be sent when available; or
   (*c*) inform you that it is no longer in print.

Design a postcard to be sent to those who have ordered the books. It should contain the information given above. If (*a*), inform the customer the book is ready for collection; if (*b*), inform him/her that you will let him/her know when it arrives; if (*c*), begin, 'We regret . . . '

The card should be suitably spaced and headed to allow you to quote the author, title and cost.

The List

Author	**Book**	**Publisher**
L. W. Burgess	The Twentieth Century Book of Crosswords	Pan
J. A. Corbett	The Essentials of Modern German Grammar	Harrap
Smith & Wilkins	The Sheldon Book of Verse, Book 3	Oxford
Rumer Godden	The Greengage Summer	Macmillan
George MacBeth (Ed.)	Poetry 1900–1965	Longman
J. L. Hanson	The Structure of Modern Commerce	Macdonald & Evans
Samuel Hayes	An Outline of Statistics (8th Edition)	Longman
Dorsch (Ed.)	English Short Stories of Today	Oxford
Smith & Keenan	English Law	Pitman
Denyer	Office Administration	Macdonald & Evans
Padfield	British Constitution Made Simple	W. H. Allen
Benemy	Whitehall – Town Hall	Harrap
R. P. Hewett	A Choice of Poets	Harrap
Harry Levin	Christopher Marlowe	Faber
J. M. Cohen (Ed.)	Penguin Book of Spanish Poets	Penguin
Charles Dickens	David Copperfield	Penguin
Bertrand Russell	A History of Western Philosophy	Unwin
Robert M. Hutchinson	The Learning Society	Pall Mall
D. B. Jackson	The Exam Secret	Elliott
A Family Doctor	How Not To Kill Yourself	Allen & Unwin
Duncan	The Fourth Dimension	Mowbray
Charles Dickens	The Old Curiosity Shop	Penguin
Karl Marx	Capital	Everyman (Dent)
Apsley Garrard	The Worst Journey in the World	Penguin
G. M. Trevelyan	History of England	Longman
William Golding	Lord of the Flies	Faber
Wm. Shakespeare	Much Ado About Nothing	Penguin

Author	Book	Publisher
	The New English Bible (Presentation Edn)	Oxford
Hans Andersen	Fairy Tales	Batsford
Wm. Shakespeare	Hamlet (School Study edn)	Longman
Wm. Shakespeare	Othello (School Study edn)	Longman
Wm. Thackeray	Vanity Fair	Macmillan
Wm. Thackeray	The History of Henry Esmond	Macmillan
The Post Office	The Post Office Guide 1979	H.M.S.O.
John Bunyan	Pilgrims Progress	Penguin
R. L. Stevenson	Travels With a Donkey	Everyman (Dent)
Peter Little	English for the Office	Longman
George Brown	In My Way	Harrap
W. Fowler	The Concise Oxford Dictionary	Oxford

Assignment No. 2

Mr. I. Wolff, the manager of the Newtown branch of the New British Office Machines Company, is going for two or three days to visit the company's head office in Manchester. The following instructions have been left for you, his private secretary.

1. On opening the mail this morning, I found three letters with the same complaint – a promised cheque had been left out of correspondence from us. Send memo to manager, accounts section – ask him to investigate and act.
2. Mrs. Smiles, one of our cleaners, has been finding cigarette ends in the washbasins in the Ladies Rooms. Also coffee (or tea?) dregs at the bottom of office waste baskets. Memo – all sections in admin. building. Smoking only in rest rooms and canteen – ashtrays. Coffee & tea – not in offices. Consideration for cleaners.
3. New car park to be opened at end of next week – Friday. One-way system. Parking spaces in front of admin. buildings – managers only. Spaces at rear of this block now for visitors. **No** private cars in factory area – for firm's vehicles only. New car park for all employees. Enough space – none reserved. Use underpass to walk from car park to main buildings and factory. For employees brought to work by car – a square to right-hand of car park entrance. Security staff will operate system. Sketch maps being prepared. Please prepare notices about this for general distribution.
4. Memo. to managers. Pay increases for all staff have been agreed and approved. Backdated four months. To be paid on first pay-day next month. Full details in pay packets on Thursday. Any enquiries to wages section after Monday next.

Assignment No. 3

The General Manager of Newtown Bus Services Ltd. has received the following letter:

28 Wood Lane,
Newtown,
Hopeshire,
NE6 7UR.

October 17th, 1980

The General Manager,
Newtown Bus Services Ltd.,
High Street,
Newtown. NE5 8XY.

Dear Sir,

Bus Services - Route 111

I wish to draw your attention to problems I have had recently concerning the buses on Route 111.

Near my home there is a request stop outside the 'Bull and Crown' public house. On Tuesday, Wednesday and Thursday last week, at 8.15 a.m., I gave a signal for the No. 111 bus to stop. It failed to do so. On Wednesday I could see quite clearly that there were unoccupied seats. I should be pleased if you would remind drivers of their duty to stop when a signal is given by a would-be passenger.

Having missed the bus on these days I had to wait one hour before the next one arrived. I feel that the peak period service on this route is insufficient and would ask that the bus company give serious thought to an improvement.

On the occasions when the bus did stop and I was able to board it I found myself being jostled and pushed around by a large number of children and college students, Some were very bad-mannered and noisy. I noticed that they were not paying fares but had a pass. Could the bus company arrange for these children to travel separately? I am sure that you could put on a special school bus or that a coach could be hired. This then would leave the buses free for the fare-paying public.

I look forward to your comments on these matters.

Yours faithfully,
(I. M. Fair)

1. Reply to this letter on behalf of the Company. Acknowledge – apologise. Paragraph 2 – bus was full on certain days – bus crews are

being reminded of the rules about request stops. Paragraph 3 – time-tables take into account availability of crews and vehicles – at present there are shortages of both – rising costs also make it hard to improve services. Paragraph 4 – passes are paid for by the Local Education Authority – no one travels free. For reasons stated above a special bus is out of the question. Other hired vehicles are arranged by the authority. Suggest that Mr. Fair write to the Local Education Authority.

2. Prepare a memo to be issued to all bus crews to remind them of the rules for bus-stops. Draw attention to the fact that a complaint has been received. Compulsory red stops – drivers must stop whether passengers are waiting there or not. Request stops – white – always stop at request of passengers inside bus – stop if someone wants to get on the bus – if there is room. If no room – acknowledge signal and indicate that you are unable to stop.
3. As Mr. (or Mrs.) Fair, follow up the suggestion that you write to the County Education Authority. Address: County Education Officer, Hopeshire County Council, County Hall, Newtown, NE1 1AA.

Assignment No. 4

On September 5th, 1980, Mrs. Sweeting purchased from Newtown Super Stores a 98-pence size 'Spray-Clene' grease and stain remover. When she got home she followed the instructions printed on the side of the container so that she could remove a grease stain on the jacket of her husband's suit. This was fairly new. A yellow looking liquid came out and formed a circular patch on and around the stain. As instructed, she left it on for 30 minutes before beginning to brush the 'Spray-Clene' off. Instead of the liquid being removed the affected area of the jacket fell away.

She went back at once to the Stores from which she bought the 'Spray-Clene'. The manager said that it was nothing to do with him. 'I didn't make it,' he stated. He merely sold the product. He advised her to return it to the manufacturers, Wonderland Domestic Products, of Bridgington. Mrs. Sweeting decided to write them a letter first.

The makers replied at once with an apology and offer to have the jacket repaired. They also asked her to send them the offending container for examination. In reply, Mrs. Sweeting said that she was returning the 'Spray-Clene' separately. She stated that she was amazed that they were only offering to repair the jacket. She had already seen the tailor from whom the suit had been bought. Additional pairs of trousers could be supplied but no jackets. Her husband would have to buy another suit. She therefore insisted that Wonderland Domestic Products pay the cost of a new suit.

Wonderland Domestic Products had the spray examined and were informed by their analyst that the company had used, inadvertently, a liquid which was harmful to fabric materials and which had reacted with the powder which was intended to be the cleaning agent. Mrs. Sweeting was informed but the company still declined to replace the suit. The company also decided to contact the wholesalers and have 'Spray-Clene' withdrawn. Refunds would be made in respect of returned goods. Mrs. Sweeting was still not satisfied and decided to go to the local office of the Citizens' Advice Bureau. The adviser expressed the view that the shopkeeper who sold the goods had some responsibility in law. He believed she might have a good case in a claim for damages and suggested that she see a solicitor. He was prepared to arrange for her to see that Bureau's solicitor. To help him she should prepare a written statement to outline what had happened. It should include details of the date of purchase and cost of the suit.

1. Prepare all the relevant correspondence between Mrs. Sweeting and Wonderland Domestic Products in relation to this episode.
2. Prepare Mrs. Sweeting's statement for the Bureau's solicitor.
3. As the Bureau's adviser prepare file notes relating to the interview with Mrs. Sweeting.

Assignment No. 5

As the personal secretary of Mr. Michael Jones, General Manager of Newtown Universal Developments, of Prince Regent Avenue, Newtown, it is your duty to arrive at 8.45 a.m. each day to open his and your offices. Each opens on to the corridor; there is also a door which links your rooms together.

On Monday, 9th October, you arrived at your usual time and went first to your own room. On opening the door you found that the room had been turned upside down. From where you were standing you could see that the contents of desk, cupboards and cabinets were scattered all over the floor. Your typewriter and other office machinery were also on the floor. You crossed into the manager's room, where similar confusion was to be seen. The door itself was already open. The windows had been broken and glass was on the floor. A small safe had been dragged across the floor and lay beneath the window. Without touching anything in those rooms you went to an office further along the corridor and from there phoned the police.

When Mr. Jones arrived and had been informed of the situation he asked you to send a Telex message to the company's head office at Western Way, London, to let the Managing Director know what had happened. A full report followed. You were asked to prepare this later in the day.

Prepare this report. It should include an account of all that you saw and did, any action that was taken by the police and a statement in detail of damage to equipment and property, of missing property and an estimate of the value of all that was damaged or that was missing. Details of missing cash and files should be given. The missing files included four confidential files containing information about new processes and modifications to plant. All files should be referred to by reference numbers.

Assignment No. 6

On a recent visit to Sandsea you bought a half-pound box of mixed chocolates at Supersales. You opened them at home two days later and found that they were not in good condition. You returned the box of chocolates to the manufacturers, Chocolate Confections Ltd., of Newtown.

1. Write the letter that will accompany them. State what action you wish to be taken.
2. Reply on behalf of the company. Thanks for letter – apologise – label in box shows that chocolates were sent out a year before – shop should not have sold them. Send separately a one-pound box straight from the factory – refund postage. Hope customer will enjoy this box and continue to buy their products.
3. From company send letter to shop which sold the chocolates – state facts. Surprise that they were on display. Request that present stock be checked – that anything more than three months old be withdrawn. Offer refund if returned within fourteen days.

Assignment No. 7

The Sales Director of Universal Stores is situated at Head Office, Newtown Way, London, W1. He has been asked to provide up-to-date sales information for a Board meeting of the company at 3.00 p.m. The time is now 9.45 a.m. He asks the Northern Sales Manager, Manchester, to send him, to arrive not later than 2.00 p.m., details of sales records for the preceding month on a week-by-week basis. For this occasion he wants the information expressed in terms of quantities sold. Under the Manchester manager are eleven area managers at Bradford, Sheffield, Preston, Chester, Liverpool, Carlisle, Sunderland, Hull, York, Scarborough and Manchester itself. To comply with the request he has to get his information from each of these. All offices are linked through the Telex system.

The following are the goods for which information is required:

Electronic

Radios:
Listener V Radio
Wonder All-wave
Miracle Pocket
Tall-Lighter Radio

Calculators:
Einstein 6 – all functions
Dinkie Compact – for handbag or wallet
Constant Service – for all office use
The Scholar

Music centres:
Northern Counties Stereo Record Player, Radio, Tape Recorder Unit complete
De Luxe Wonderland

Tape recorders:
Listener Tape Model IV
Bijou Pocket Recorder

Domestic

Food mixers:
Splodge Special Complete
Universal Blendermatic

Electric knife sharpener:

Barbecues:
Unibarb Electric
Primitbarb – oil heated unit

Dishwashing machines:
Family Model
Manor House Marvel
Wonder Work
New Servant Model

Freezers and refrigerators:
Tall Boy (Freezer and Refrigerator)
Small Universal Freezer
Medium Universal Freezer
Large Universal Freezer
Arctic Slim Refrigerator
Alaska Family Refrigerator

1. Produce a sales catalogue listing the above. Alphabetical order of sections, sub-sections and models should be used. The catalogue will be for the use of the managers and staff of all the Northern area offices and branches of Universal Stores. Columns should be headed to show catalogue number references, the recommended price of each article, the stores' retail price, VAT and total selling

price. Give each item listed a catalogue reference number.
2. Prepare the Telex message from Head Office to Manchester.
3. Prepare the Telex message from Manchester to one of the area offices.
4. Prepare the Telex reply of that office to Manchester.
5. Assume that figures for all areas have been received at Manchester. (The student should invent these for the purpose of this activity.) Prepare Manchester's final Telex to London.
6. Using the information given in 5, above, prepare a suitable table to be presented to each member of the Board meeting.

Assignment No. 8

Newtown Market Development — Actors' Theatre

The Newtown District Council has approved plans for the construction of a new covered market over which will be built accommodation for shops and stores. Two storeys above the market are provided for. In diagram I (Fig. 4) this scheme will involve the areas G, H, J and F. Area G is at present in use as an open car park. Area F is a piece of waste-land which is used on occasions as an emergency car park. H is the site of a large dance hall and licensed premises. J. consistes of a row of shops.

The proposals are set out in diagram II (Fig. 5). The buildings on area H will be demolished and the new covered market will extend across F and G. The section of Telford Crescent between Macadam Street and the theatre will be closed and a new one constructed. This is shown shaded with oblique lines in diagram II and is to be named Market Crescent. It will provide access to the market and will be open to traffic only during market hours, at present on four days only. A narrower road offering limited access to the theatre, church and college is shown with grey shading. This road and area will have permanent, no-parking restrictions except that it may be used by the church for the purpose of weddings and funerals only. A pedestrian footpath from West Road will provide access to the college, church and theatre and then through either to the town centre or to some ornamental gardens.

A document giving full details of all the proposals has been circulated to all present users of the open market, which will be closed when the new one is opened, to occupiers of adjacent premises and of the affected area, to the management of the theatre, the rector of the church and the principal of Newtown College of Science and Technology. The proposals have been submitted to the Hopeshire County Council as the planning authority.

A meeting of the Supporters' Club of the Newtown Actors' Theatre

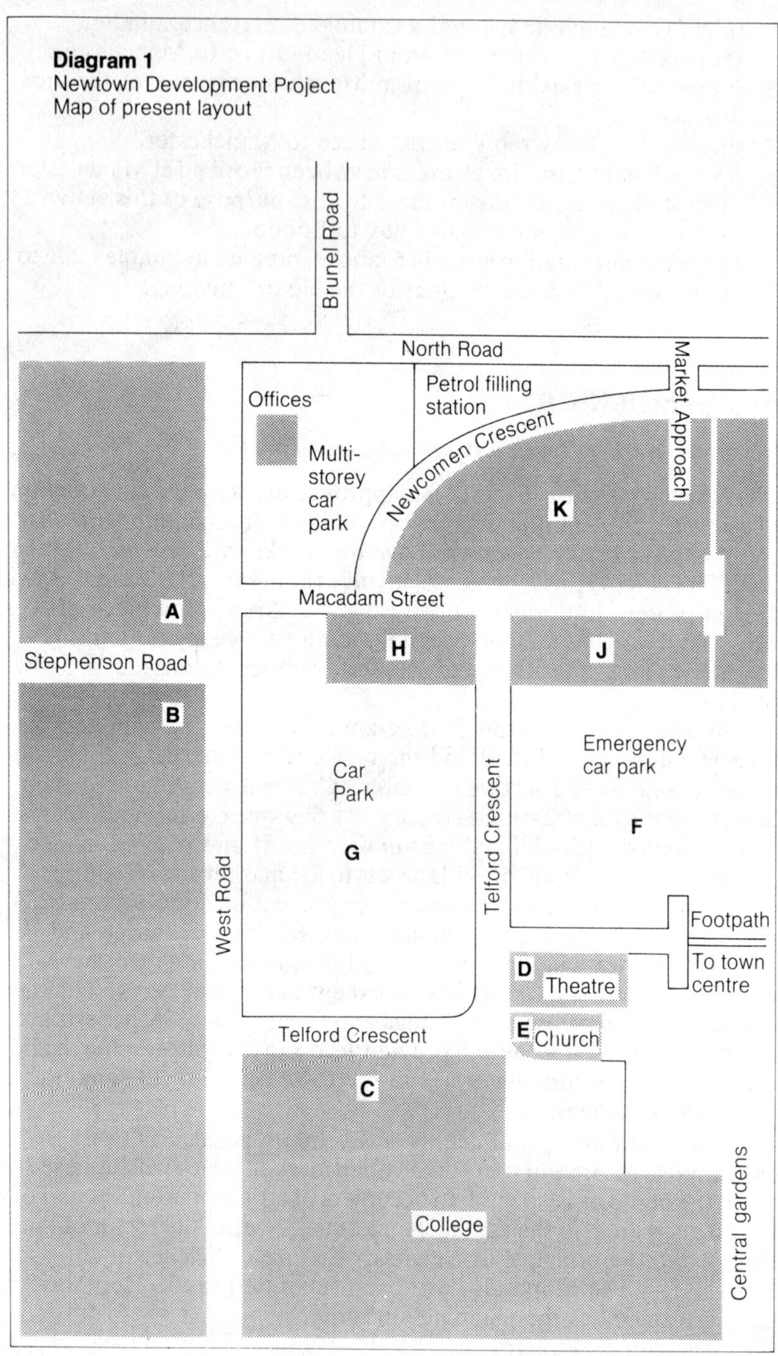
Diagram 1
Newtown Development Project
Map of present layout
Brunel Road
North Road
Market Approach
Offices
Petrol filling station
Newcomen Crescent
Multi-storey car park
K
A
Macadam Street
Stephenson Road
H
J
B
Emergency car park
Car Park
Telford Crescent
F
G
West Road
Footpath
To town centre
D
Theatre
E
Church
Telford Crescent
C
College
Central gardens

Fig. 4

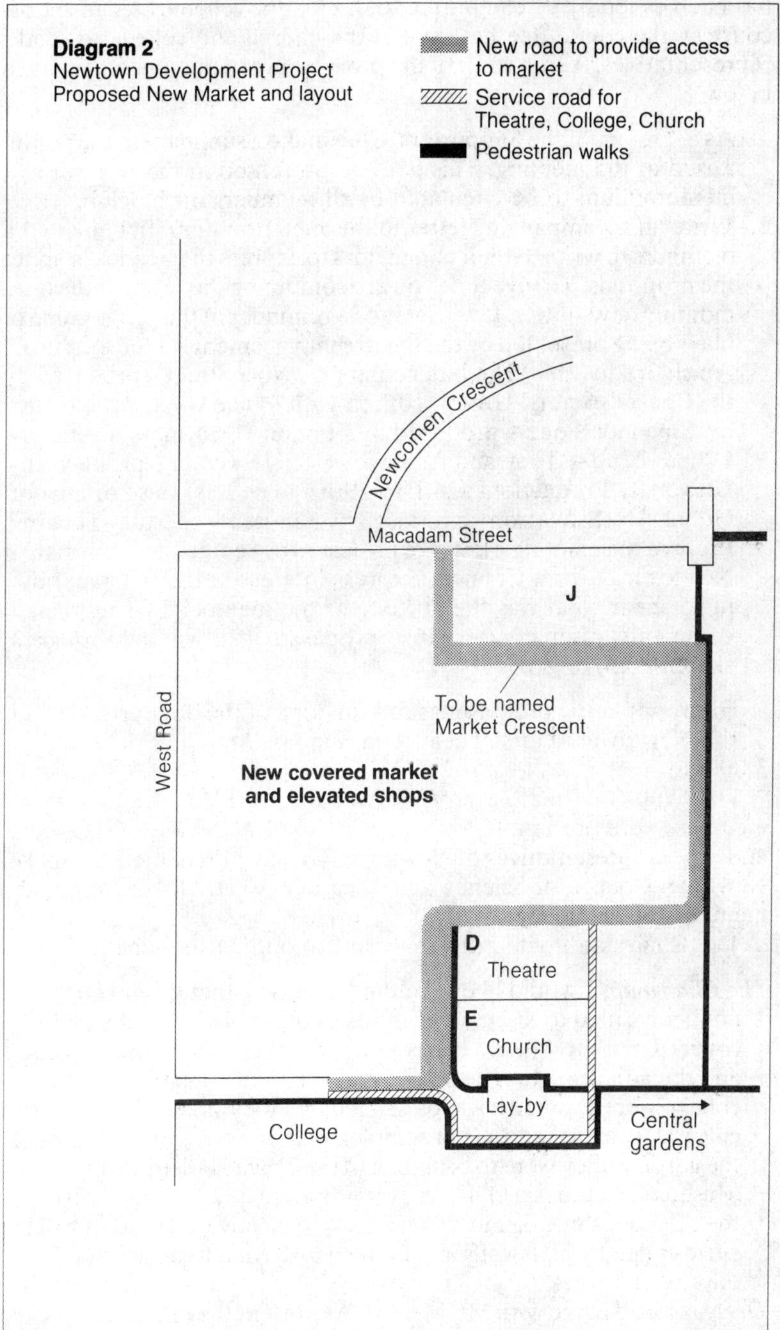
Diagram 2
Newtown Development Project
Proposed New Market and layout
New road to provide access to market
Service road for Theatre, College, Church
Pedestrian walks
Newcomen Crescent
Macadam Street
J
To be named Market Crescent
West Road
New covered market and elevated shops
D
Theatre
E
Church
Lay-by
College
Central gardens

Fig. 5

has been called by its committee to discuss the scheme. As an act of courtesy the committee has invited the church and college to send representatives. A transcript of the proceedings of this meeting is given below.

1. As Secretary of the Supporters' Club make a summary of the points raised at the meeting. This is to be presented in the form of a memorandum to be circulated to all members of the club.
2. Write an accompanying letter to this memorandum. In it invite the members to write to their councillors to express their concern about the proposals. To save time you are combining this letter with your monthly news-letter. It will include a reminder of the programme of plays being presented by the theatre management for the month of April: 3rd to 8th – 'The Latecomers' by Noel Street – produced by the Coastal Actors' Group; 10th to 15th – 'The Ivy and the Holly' by Amanada Pope – produced by London Performers' Company; 17th to 22nd – 'Time and Again' by Cecily Sweeter – produced by University Productions; 24th to 29th – 'The Last Case of Doctor Holmes' by S. Watson – produced by Sandsea Repertory Theatre.
3. Prepare the meeting's letter of protest to be sent to the Chairman of Newtown District Council. Express interest in the scheme, but make clear what was the attitude of the members. Using their comments, offer some positive proposals. If it will help to use a sketch-map, do so.

Transcript of the proceedings of a meeting of the Supporters' Club of the Newtown Actors' Theatre on Sunday, March 15th, 1980, at 3.00 p.m.

The Club Chairman, Mr. V. C. Merritt, presided. About 150 members were present. In addition were the Rector, Rev. G. Goode, and other representatives of Newtown Parish Church, the Principal of Newtown College of Science and Technology, Dr. J. Newton, and members of the college staff.

The Chairman invited the Secretary to outline the scheme.

The Chairman: I would like to remind members that this meeting has not been called to discuss the merits or otherwise of a scheme for a covered market. We are here to examine their effect on our theatre and the adjacent church and college. When the theatre, church and college were planned it was envisaged that they should form part of a cultural, spiritual and social complex in the Town Centre. Through the gardens they were to be linked to the Town Hall, the Library, the Museum and the Art Gallery. This proposed new complex will have the effect of shutting our theatre away. The covered market will be surrounded by high walls and flanked by a road to be used on four days of the week.

Dr. Newton: I agree with Mr. Merritt. At present the main entrance to the college faces the church and is easily found. When the new complex is built visitors are going to have difficulty in finding it. The present space in front of the college entrance provides adequate parking for visitors. Under the new plans this area is to be the subject of 'No Parking' regulations. This will prove to be a strain on our other parking facilities in the college. Visitors will have to park at the Newcomen multi-storey car park and walk from there to the college. I suggest that the District Council seriously consider allowing the college to continue to use the quadrangle in front of the main entrance.

Rev. R. Goode: We are all going to be dwarfed by this new structure. I am very worried about the proposals for the high wall, unused road and adjacent footpath. Our church is in use throughout the week as well as on Sundays. We have activities each evening. There is every possibility that this could become an ill-lit area attracting undesirables.

Mrs. S. Smith: Two of my daughters are in the Guides. I may have to withdraw them if they have to walk along this footpath in the dark.

Mr. J. Thomas: My daughter is in the evening typing class at college. This new road will encourage thugs and muggers. When she leaves college she will have to cross the service road and face the danger of traffic on a very narrow road.

Mr. S. Cooke (Catering Manager at the Theatre): Quite a number of people use our restaurants every day. I understand that the new market will have a large self-service restaurant on the upper level. This will take our day trade. In the evening the restricted access will stop many of our regulars attending.

Mr. E. Wise: Wherever there are markets there is rubbish – and muck as well. Neither of these is very attractive, except to tramps and scavengers.

Mr. S. Jones: I think the Council ought to think again about the road. Why can't they keep the present road? They could, if need be, build their market buildings over it.

Cries – No – this will be worse. The road would then be dark. It would be easier for people to hide in the shadows.

Various people suggested that the new road should remain open at all times.

Mr. L. Smith: I think it's a shame to hide our theatre.

Mr. S. Jones: I would like to propose that we tell the Council that we disapprove of the scheme as far as it affects us – that we want the road left open.

Mr. S. Cook: Yes, and make it clear that we want the road to be well lit.

Finally, it was agreed that the Secretary should write to the Newtown District Council to express as strongly as possible the feelings of the Supporters' Club.

Assignment No. 9

Recently there have been staff changes at Electrical and Mechanical Products, Newtown. As a result the personnel department has been dealing with many queries about the company's services and benefits for its staff.

The management has agreed that all the available information should be collated and printed in the form of a memorandum to be distributed to all employees, displayed on all notice-boards and filed for reference in each section. As the personal secretary of the Senior Personnel Officer you have been asked to do this and prepare a draft copy for approval.

These are the Personnel Officer's notes:

Breakdown:
Holidays
Sickness – including pay*
Training facilities
Staff canteens
Social – club – sports ground
*Also other absences – domestic – special occasions. This also links with Flexitime.

S. *Leave of absence with pay** – for first 6 weeks. Half pay up to 12 weeks. Thereafter subject to medical review board.
* Medical certificate required after 3 days.

H. *After 1 yr. service 3 wks. paid.* (1 wk. = 5 working days. S & Su excluded.) At 5 yrs. service + 1 wk. Over 10 yrs. + 2 wks. Start of year 2nd Jan – no carry-over to following year. Bank hols. extra. Under 1 yr. service 1 day per month for first 9 months. After that – up to 12 months full 3 weeks.

C. *Basement canteen – snacks – light meals.** 11–12.30. Sun Restaurant – top floor – 2–3 course meals. Wines. 11.30–3.00. Concession rates – see boards – for all staff. *Self service. In restroom on each floor – tea, coffee, biscuits 9.45–10.00, 12–2.00, 3.14–4.00. N.B. Morning & afternoon break 20 mins per person. Lunch time – see Flexitime.

T. *Under 20 – day release to College.* 1 day. Course to be approved by T.O. Over 20 – day release – approved Higher courses – generally related to Electrical, Production Engineering, Secretarial, Computer, Accountancy, Management. Fees – books. (Claim on Form T.F.) Exam fees – refund if successful.
Where approved, fees or assistance for evening or correspondence. If in connection with firm's business, company will finance attendance at short courses of up to 1 week. (T.O. = Training Officer.)

Social. Electrical & Mechanical Products Social Club. Open to all staff. Annual subs. £2.50. Husbands/wives may become associates, £1.50. Clubhouse – bars – restaurants. Badminton – squash – indoor table games. Open daily – lunch time 12–2.30. Evening 5.30 to closing time. Other clubs – on main premises. Details on boards. Occasional social evenings – discos – dances – etc. Information from Social Club Sec. – Miss E. Games. Ext. 246. Sales & Accts. Section. Clubhouse – SURROUNDED BY Sports Ground. Sports Sec. John Champion – ext. 139.

Flexitime. Core time 10.00 to 3.30. Flexibands 8.00 to 10.00 and 3.30 to 5.30. Lunch time 1 hour within 12 to 2.30 Individuals to be in during core time. Other time within flexibands. Within 4 week period must work total of 140 contract hours. By arrangement with section leaders time may be built up – 2 half days off in any one week. Scheme caters for all domestic, personal & emergencies. To help calculate time worked – all to clock in & out daily.

Assignment No. 10

A sudden rise in temperature at the end of April caused an equally sudden demand for ice-cream products in Essex. Within two days the shops had exhausted their supplies – two days later the Essex supply depot for Tasti-Creme was out of stock. An urgent Telex had to be sent to the main factory at Bristol from the Chelmsford depot for the following: 2,000 boxes Milk Choc Ices; 2,000 boxes Plain Choc Ices; 500 boxes each Strawberry, Raspberry, Lemon, Orange Lollies; 300 boxes Tasti-Sun Specials; 400 boxes Southern Sky Sundaes; 1,000 2-litre containers Dairy Cream, Vanilla, Strawberry, Peach soft scoop ice-creams.

Compose this Telex (ask for time van leaves Bristol). Also prepare reply from Bristol. Answer-backs: Telex nos. + Tasti-Essex or Tasti-Bristol.

Assignment No. 11

You work in the Sales Section of Happy Gifts Ltd., where you deal with outstanding debts. You are at its Head Office, at 1 Central Buildings, London, EC4 2XX.

The customers, whose names are shown below, have outstanding amounts. The debts were contracted at various branches of the firm. Each customer has received, in addition to the original invoice, three reminders to pay. The firm's copy of the invoice was signed when he or she received the goods.

A letter, strongly worded, is now to be sent to each to draw attention to the continued non-payment. Full details of the account and correspondence have now been sent to the company's solicitors, Messrs Bailey, Justice and Fines, of Judgement Lane, London EC1. They have been instructed to take necessary action to recover the debts. All future correspondence must now be addressed to the solicitors.

	Amount (£)	Invoice No	Date of Invoice
Mr. Dunne	45.65	ST 4691	10/8/79
Mr. Speedy	47.89	ST 6508	12/7/79
Miss Spendthrift	67.44	ST 7171	24/6/79
Mrs Clerverley	72.30	SX 0405	1/8/79
Mr. Mechanic	46.99	SX 0516	12/8/79
Miss Liverdene	45.33	SP 0721	5/8/79
Mr. Freezy	72.72	SX 0888	18/8/79
Mr. Slowcombe	54.85	SY 0748	5/8/79
Mr. Golightly	59.18	SA 0101	2/8/79
Miss Heavy	88.16	SA 0211	8/8/79

1. Draft the letter to be sent to each of the customers. For Mr. Freezy see below.
2. Write the letter from the company to the solicitors.
   (*a*) Include the list given above, arranged in chronological order of dates of transaction. Where there is more than one transaction on the same date, arrange in alphabetical order of customers.
   (*b*) Enclose copies of the invoices.
   (Prepare one invoice, that for Mr. Freezy. Goods bought: 1 'Cheerful' Radio Transistor, £24.75. 4 Batteries, £1.40. 4 L.P. Records, £15.27. 1 Tape Recorder, £31.30. Purchased at Newtown Branch, 6 High Street.)
   (*c*) State facts and instruct them to take all necessary action to recover the debt.
3. Compose the letter that the solicitors would send to Mr. Freezy.
   (*a*) Repeat your instructions from the company – state facts about debt.
   (*b*) Give final date by which account is to be settled – three weeks from date of solicitor's letter.
   (*c*) Future communications must be with the solicitors, not the firm.
   (*d*) Failure to conform – summons to attend County Court will be issued.

Assignment No. 12

Mr. and Mrs. Sharpe arrived home together from work on Thursday, October 11th, 1980, at 5.15 p.m., to find a ticket left by the Newtown Station branch of the Railway Express Parcels Delivery Service. It indicated that a packet had been left in the porch of their house. Their house has no porch and there was no packet. Mr. Sharpe checked with neighbours to find out if the packet had been left with them by mistake. It had not. Mrs. Sharpe decided to telephone the station. The following conversation took place:

R. This is Newtown Station Parcels Office.
Mrs. S. When I got home a short while ago I found a card on the floor to say that you had left a packet in the porch. There is no porch and there is no packet.
R. That's no business of mine. The packet has been delivered.
Mrs. S. I haven't received it. You shouldn't have left it at the door-step.
R. It's your lookout if you choose to go to work instead of staying in for parcels. This place is cluttered up with undelivered and unclaimed parcels. Some have been here for months.
Mrs. S. Why couldn't the vanman have brought my parcel back?
R. We don't want these undelivered parcels all over the place.
Mrs. S. It's your responsibility. What are you going to do about it?
R. Nothing. We've delivered it. If it has gone you'd better tell the police.
Mrs. S. Isn't it possible the driver carried the parcel back to the van? Can't you check?
R. The van's out. It won't be back till 6.30. You'd better ring in the morning.
Mrs. S. I will – but if it's not there I shall not let it rest.

Later that evening, at 6.15, Mrs. Sharpe was called to collect her daughter at the station. She decided to check for the packet.

Mrs. S. I've called to see if a packet has been brought back.
R. Were you on the phone earlier? You said you would ring in the morning. The van's not back yet.

The following morning Mrs. Sharpe rang the parcels office. A different person was on duty. He confirmed that the van had returned but without the packet. He said that the entry on the vanman's sheet for the package referred to – serial number 110068 – had the entry 'delivered to the house'. As far as the railway were concerned it was now out of their hands. He too said that Mrs. Sharpe should contact the police. At her request he informed her that the package had been sent by Wondertoys Ltd., of Brightlingstone, East Anglia.

Mr. and Mrs. Sharpe decided to inform the police in writing. He wrote the letter. He also wrote a letter to the General Manager, Anglian Region, British Railways, London, EC, to report the loss and express his feelings very strongly about the policy of leaving parcels outside houses and failing to obtain signatures. He stressed that railways have a duty to people who entrust them with packages to deliver.

Mrs. Sharpe has ordered and paid for the goods from Wondertoys. She wrote a letter to inform them that her order had not yet arrived.

1. Compose each of these letters – add any information that you think should be given; for example, date of order to Wondertoys, cheque number. Conversations should be summarised into reported speech.
2. The General Manager sends to Stationmaster, Newtown, for a report. It should include summaries of statements from Parcels Office staff and the vanman.
3. Compose an appropriate reply from the General Manager to Mr. & Mrs. Sharpe. Advise them to contact Wondertoys.
4. Letter from Wondertoys. Package sent. If it does not turn up within 14 days – inform them. Another package will be sent or money refunded as desired.
5. Newtown police send a detective constable to interview the Sharpes.
   Reconstruct the interview and write it out in a similar form to the conversation given at the beginning. The police are basically investigating what could be called a theft. They will be concerned to know the details of the order (goods and value), evidence that the package was left at the house, discovery that it was missing, steps taken to find out if it had gone elsewhere. Acting as the detective constable, construct a suitable statement to be signed by one of the Sharpes. The statement should begin with these words,

   'This statement, consisting of . . . sheets, each signed by me, is, to the best of my knowledge and belief, true. I am aware that it may be used as evidence and understand that if any of it is false I may be liable to prosecution'.

   It is usual for the official form used by the police to contain spaces in the heading for full name, address, age and occupation of the person making the statement.

Assignment No. 13

Mr. M. Singer, of 14 Hadrian's Crescent, Bordertown, Cumbria, has been suffering recently from headaches. His doctor advised him to visit his optician, Dr. J. Oculist. The latter, after examining him, informed him that he needs to wear glasses, both for distance vision and for reading. After discussion, Mr. Singer agreed to have glasses fitted with multi-focal lenses, made by Varigrade Focal Lenses Ltd. He was asked to sign a green form, part of which Dr. Oculist had completed. On this part Dr. Oculist stated that he had examined Mr. Singer, recommended the wearing of glasses and completed details of a prescription for the glasses. Mr. Singer was told that the form would be returned to him and that he must bring it back to the optician who would then arrange to have the glasses made.

On the following day, Mr. Singer heard from his employer, the Inland Revenue Department of the Civil Service, that he was to be transferred two weeks later to Portville, in Sussex. He went to see Dr. Oculist who suggested that when the green form was returned Mr. Singer should take it to Clearsight Ltd., Opticians in Portville.

The green form was received before Mr. Singer left. When he had arrived in Portville he did not take the form to Clearsight but went instead, after listening to a neighbour, to New Optics. The neighbour convinced him that New Optics were much better opticians. Three weeks later his spectacles arrived. When he tried them the distance element of the lenses was satisfactory, but he found the reading part gave blurred vision. The assistant suggested that this was because he had never previously worn glasses. He told Mr. Singer that he would get used to it. He paid for them and took them away. At work he found that they were not helpful and that he still had his headache. He went back to New Optics to be told that nothing could be done. He had signed to say that the glasses were satisfactory. The assistant suggested that he could have another eye test by their specialist.

He talked the matter over with his supervisor at work, who advised him to write to the Sussex Health Executive, at Brighton. He did this and was asked in reply to take or send the spectacles to the Executive at Brighton to be examined. He sent them by registered post and, in an accompanying letter, asked that they be returned speedily as he had got used to the distance element.

When examined, the glasses were found not to conform to the original prescription. A letter was sent to New Optics. In reply this company disagreed with the Executive's reading of the prescription. It added that the specialist was not one for whom it normally dispensed and pointed out that his writing was not easy to read. The prescription had been copied out by one of its optical assistants. The Executive wrote to Dr. Oculist and asked him to inform them of the correct prescription. His reply showed the prescription to be as the Executive had interpreted it.

The Executive sent another letter to New Optics. It repeated its reading of the prescription. The following points were added – if in doubt consult the specialist who had issued the prescription – a qualified technical optician should check the work of clerical assistants – a patient's signature did not remove the optician's duty to supply the correct lenses. Instruct New Optics to make new lenses – no extra cost to Mr. Singer. Failure would lead to a deduction from the Executive's payments to the company.

The complainant to be informed of decision and instructed to take his glasses back for new lenses. He should write to the Executive if he had further difficulties.

The student should prepare all correspondence relating to this matter.

Address:
New Optics – 4 Long Way, Portville.
Mr. Singer (new address) – 15 Weald Way, Portville.
Dr. J. Oculist – 20 Augusta Road, Bordertown.

Assignment No. 14

Major Footwear has taken over premises at 46–48 High Street, Newtown, which it is now adapting and fitting out.

On June 10th it was decided to make the opening date a grand publicity occasion. Miss Greater Europe is to be invited to perform the opening ceremony. A publicity leaflet giving details of the opening will be distributed to householders in Newtown. A special reception committee will meet Miss Greater Europe at Newtown Station about an hour or so before the ceremony. An approach is to be made to a local firm, Happy Wedding Coaches Ltd., which hires out for weddings a coach and two pairs of horses, accompanied by footmen. The special visitor would be conveyed from the station to the town centre in this way.

You have been given administrative responsibility for the whole project and have listed the following tasks to be done:

1. Write to Miss Greater Europe's agents, Eldorado Leisure Entertainments, London W1 to invite her. Give a detailed statement of her itinerary. Train arrives at 9.50 a.m. The opening at 11.30 a.m. Lunch at the Prince Albert Hotel at 12.25 p.m. If she wishes – a conducted tour of Newtown. State other personalities who may be present (include Chairman of Newtown Council, local M.P. and others). Include a short summary account of Major Footwear – its history, range of goods sold, any specialisation. Ask about fees and request any publicity material.
2. Letters are to be sent to the Chairman of Newtown District Council and to the M.P. Invite them to lunch as well. Remember to give them an outline of the programme.
3. Write the letter to Happy Wedding Coaches Ltd. to arrange for the hire of carriage, horses and footmen to bring Miss Greater Europe from the station.
4. When Eldorado Leisure Entertainments have agreed that she can come, write to Miss Greater Europe a personal letter of thanks and promise further details later. Her agents have sent you her address.
5. A list of people to be invited has been drawn up. Prepare an invitation card to be sent to each.
6. Prepare the publicity leaflet.
7. Inform press of arrangements. Personal invitation to the editor.

8. Final letter to be sent to Miss Greater Europe

On September 25th you are told that the display cabinets have not arrived. Your contractors, Shop Conversions, Ltd., are very apologetic because they forgot to order any. You should contact the manufacturers by Telex. They are Display Furniture Manufacturers of Gibbons Avenue, Leetown. Give an order, explain the situation and request urgent delivery by mid-day, September 27th, at the latest. Items: 3 'Super' Display Cabinets, height 8 feet – 2 open front 'Window' Cabinets, long size – 2 corner display units. The last should be designed to have a 'Calculator' cash register on top. Ask to be advised of despatch and request cost of these.

You have expressed your feelings about this let-down to the foreman of Shop Conversions working at your premises. Follow this up with a strongly worded, but polite, letter to the firm's general manager.

Finally, after the event, settle with Miss Greater Europe's agents, and send the appropriate thank-you letters.

Miss Greater Europe is Mlle. Françoise Chantreuse. She speaks and writes good English.

Assignment No. 15

Mr. Spring was employed by Newtown Electronics Ltd. as a production fitter at a rate of £2.40 an hour for a 40-hour week. The working hours are 8.30 to 12.30 and 13.30 to 17.30 daily on Mondays to Fridays. Any hours worked outside these on weekdays are paid at one and a half times the normal rate. If a person works on Saturday or Sunday he is paid twice the basic rate for all hours worked. For lateness or short hours pay is stopped on the basis of 5-minute units.

For two weeks Mr. Spring's time schedule was:

Monday	27 Feb.	8.30–12.30	13.30–18.45*
Tuesday	28 Feb.	8.40–12.30	13.30–18.50*
Wednesday	1 March	8.30–12.30	13.30–17.30
Thursday	2 March	8.45–12.30	13.30–19.30*
Friday	3 March	8.30–12.30	NOT IN
Saturday	4 March	10.00–14.00	14.30–16.30
Sunday	5 March	10.00–14.00	14.30–15.30

*½ hour tea – not paid.

Monday	6 March	8.30–12.30	13.30–19.00
Tuesday	7 March	9.00–12.30	13.30–17.30
Wednesday	8 March	8.30–12.30	13.30–17.30
Thursday	9 March	9.00–12.30	13.45–17.45*
Friday	10 March	8.30–12.30	13.30–18.00

* He agreed to treat this as normal time.

In accordance with the firm's regulations he gave notice to resign on Friday, March 3rd. These required four weeks' notice so that his last date was Friday, March 31st. In the current year, which began on the preceding April 1st, he had taken no annual leave. He will have been employed by the firm for three years on 3rd April. A copy of the holiday regulations is given as an appendix.

Because he was going on holiday the firm agreed to give him, when he left on Friday, March 10th, his wages paid up to March 31st. His gross salary was recorded as £554.40. The appropriate stoppages for income tax and national insurance were also made.

On April 7th, he wrote to his General Manager and made the following points.

1. March 24th and March 27th were Bank Holidays and they were not included in holidays. Ought he to have had more pay?
2. He thought he was underpaid by £10, apart from this.
3. His income tax code read 140 on his pay slip. It should have been 155, according to his coding notice. He wanted the firm to refund the overpaid tax.

The Manager referred the letter to the Wages Department, which made these observations.

1. Agreed – these dates were omitted. Send a cheque, but tax will have to be stopped. Now new tax year – firm has not got his records – tax will have to be stopped for Emergency rate.
2. Firm was correct – send copy of weekly wages analysis.
3. An error – tax records have gone to the tax office. He must contact them – suggest he takes with him P.45 and Coding Notice. Wages Dept. will write to tax office. Manager asked for letter to be drafted.

1. Compose Mr. Spring's letter.
2. Prepare Manager's letter to Mr. Spring.
3. Prepare Wage's letter to Mr. Spring.
4. Using information in Mr. Spring's time sheet, prepare a suitable weekly wages sheet. The following information should be included: days worked – number of basic hours (deduct late, etc.) – number of weekday overtime hours – number of weekend overtime hours. Provide space for Income Tax, National Insurance and any other stoppages. Complete, as far as possible, these sheets for Mr. Spring for remainder of his time with firm from 27th February.
5. Prepare a suitable letter of protest from Mr. Spring to indicate his reaction to the Manager's letter.

Appendix

Extract from holiday regulations.

The entitlement of staff to holiday with pay is:

1. For staff during their first year with the company,
   1 day's paid holiday for each month worked.
   3 days' paid leave for the twelfth, making a total for the year of 14 days.
2. For staff with the company for up to 4 years,
   3 weeks' paid annual leave after the first year.
3. For staff with the company over 4 years,
   4 weeks' paid annual leave.
   N.B. – 1 week is equivalent to 5 working days.

All paid leave will be at the basic rates of pay.
The leave commences on March 1st.

Assignment No. 16

The Leicestershire Metal Company urgently requires 300 tons of zinc ore. Through its Head Office in London it contacts the European Non-Ferrous Metals Marketing Consortium, at 26 Rue Napoleon, Paris. (Telex answerback codes: Leicester Metal Co. – Dialling code number, followed by Lemeto, London: the European Consortium – Eurofermat, Paris.) A reply is received in London at 10.30 a.m., that the ore is available at Duisberg, Germany. The cost – 1150DM per ton (3.65DM = £1). Acceptance must be notified to Paris by 3.45 p.m., local time.

The next step is to contact the Shipping Agents, The North Sea Shipping Agency, London (Telex answerback code – Norship, London), to find out shipping details. The reply indicates that the British cargo vessel, S.S. 'British Admiral', registered at Harwich in 1970, is at present loading at Rotterdam. This should be completed by tomorrow. There will be enough space for the zinc ore. The 'British Admiral' should arrive at Bremerhaven at about 6.00 a.m., local time the day after. The ore can be carried by train from Duisberg to Bremerhaven to arrive by midnight tomorrow provided instructions are received by 2.30 p.m., British Summer Time.

Insurance cover has next to be arranged. Contact must be made with Leicestershire Metal's usual insurance broker, Sealane Insurance Brokers, London. (Telex number and Sealane, London.) It requires to know details of the consignment, its value, the name and place and date of the boat's registration and the ports between which the ore will travel. The boat from Bremerhaven will go to Harwich. From there the ore will go by British Rail to Leicester. The company has a special railway siding.

The Insurance Broker contacts the Major Insurance Company, which offers, as lead insurer, a quotation of 2% of the value of the ore. The Minor Insurance Company offers a quotation as follower of 1%. Sealane communicates these quotations and adds its own ½%

commission. Sealane Insurance Brokers also arrange for John Bull Insurance to provide insurance cover for the rail journeys at each end at the standard total rates of 1% of the value.

Finally, Leicestershire Metal sends details of the arrangements by Telex to the Harwich Port Offices of the section of the Department of Trade and Industry dealing with imports and requests permission to import the ore. The appropriate forms will be completed and sent immediately. It states that the European Non-Ferrous Metals has asked for a reply by 3.45 Paris time and the shipping company wants details by 2.30 B.S.T.

The Department of Trade replies by Telex giving provisional permission – subject to forms being in order and to payment of all dues to British Customs.

Leicestershire Metal now confirms arrangements by Telex with European Non-Ferrous Metals, the North Sea Shipping Agency and the Sealane Insurance Brokers. It also informs European Non-Ferrous Metals of the import licence reference number issued by the Department of Trade and Industry DT1/HARWICH/418/followed by the date of issue.

All communications in this assignment will be made by Telex.

Assignment No. 17

Towards the end of October Stelluna Toys Company released on to the wholesale and retail toy trade its latest model, the Brightstar, a miniature racing capsule. Four colours were available: blue, green, red and yellow.

Two days after Christmas reports came in that children in four towns, Bordertown, Oldchester, Portville and Sandsea, had been admitted to hospital suffering from unusual stomach pains. During the week that followed the conclusion was reached that the pains had been caused by paint – from the red Brightstar. Inquiries showed that each of the children involved had received a red Brightstar for Christmas. Somehow they had managed to get the red paint into their mouths.

Stelluna Toys submitted these models for examination. The firm's chemical analyst reported that the red models had been painted with a red lead-based paint, which he identified as being the same as that in tins in the stock room. These had been bought in connection with the forthcoming decoration of the administration block.

The supervisor of the section producing the Brightstar said that his section had run short of the red paint and that he himself had gone to the paint stores to collect some more. The store's assistant was not there. The supervisor saw what he thought was the paint and, on his own initiative, took some back to his section. He did not sign for what he had taken. The store's assistant had not noticed that some of the paint for decorating had gone.

Stelluna decided, as a matter of extreme urgency, to recall from the wholesalers and retailers all stocks of the red Brightstars. An appeal would also be made to the general public for the return of all red models. The chemical analyst had stressed in his report that the other colours gave no cause for worry and anxiety. As the toys had also been distributed in the Common Market it was decided to seek the co-operation of their distributing agent, 'Les Joux Internationales' of Paris.

The following tasks should be done.

1. Prepare a report to the General Manager from the chemical analyst.
2. The manager asked the supervisor of the production section for a written statement, in a report form, of what had happened to cause this mishap. Prepare this.
3. A letter is to be sent to every wholesaler and retailer to whom this particular toy had been sold. The situation should be outlined. All stocks of the **red** model must be returned. The firm will refund money that has been paid for the toys and expenses incurred. Retailers are to be asked to display a window notice and insert an advertisement in the local press to ask customers to return any red models. Copies of the window notice and press advertisements are to be enclosed. They will promise a refund to customers of money paid or offer an alternative colour.
4. Prepare:
   (*a*) the window notice;
   (*b*) the advertisement for the local paper.
5. Send a Telex message to the French agent.
6. Prepare a memorandum to be circulated to all staff concerning procedure for drawing anything from stores.
7. Write a letter of sympathy to the parents of the children – one example will do. Show sympathy but at this stage make no promises.

Assignment No. 18

Mr. Smith has recently returned from a meeting of business executives where one of the topics for discussion was the legislation on health and safety at work. This prompted him to have a quick check at his own offices and factory. He saw enough to worry him and asked the Deputy Manager, Miss Landson, to carry out an investigation in the Administration section of the premises and report back to him as soon as possible. This section is housed on two floors, the ground floor containing reception, typing rooms and rooms for senior staff. The second floor contains mainly the accounts and stores.

As she went round she made the following notes:

Ground Floor: Reception. Three large bags of waste material across the exit door. Two screws missing from wall switch panel, which is now falling away from the wall. It could easily be wrenched off. Dangerous. 'No Smoking' notices – yet four people smoking, including one security officer. A young woman walked across reception hall, carrying a long carriage typewriter which obscured her vision. She was from Sales Section – she had been sent to bring one across. Had not heard of trolleys.

Typing rooms: 3 machines plugged in, 2 switched on, but not in use. Joan Easy having difficulty with her electric typewriter – poking around in it with a steel knitting needle. She was trying 'to put it right'. Supervisor of typing section, Miss S. Hand, trying to make electric duplicator work – fingers between rollers and power switched on. Gangways obstructed by typists' coats and bags – difficult to move out if a fire. Fire procedure notices not to be seen. Jane Shakespeare, age 16, standing tip-toe on edge of chair, reaching up above her head trying to lift about 8 files, all quite full, from the shelf above her. Could just reach bottom file with fingers. Filing cabinets not in use but drawers open. In one case a drawer open just above a typist's head.

Fire exit stairs from room above. Fire doors open and fastened back. Boxes of documents, dust laden, stacked on landings between each flight of steps (N.B. storage space in basement). No electric bulb on second landing.

Second Floor: Accounts room. Broken windows – glass on floor – at least two weeks old. (Cleaners. Are they doing their job?) Window open – a clerk, Alan Burston, leaning right out. Typewriter trolley filled with ledgers. Service lift – iron gate wide open. Lift at floor above. Two people playing about in the area – one a typist from below – one an office boy.

Stores: Spirit room (duplication spirit). Accounts girl, Judith Golfer, having a smoke – 'didn't see sign'. Paper store room. A gallon can of petrol there. Put in by George Walker, a male accounts clerk. 'I was leaving it there till I went home.'

On ground floor: One fire bucket missing. Two needed to be filled. Sand buckets not on hook provided. One fire extinguisher missing.

On second floor: One water bucket only. Sand bucket in middle of accounts clerks section – used for cigarette ends. Fire hoses had been pulled out. Seen from upstairs window – direction signs below being ignored by car drivers. The Purchasing Manager drove out against a 'No Entry' sign.

Miss Landson will use these notes to make a formal report to Mr. Smith. She proposes that a general memorandum be drawn up on the subject of safety and circulated to all members of the firm. Also she suggests a meeting of section supervisors and managers. She thinks that Mr. Smith himself should see those whom she had named.

1. Draw up Miss Landson's formal report.

2. Using this material produce a memorandum on the subject of 'Safety at Work'. It should deal with general principles rather than the mistakes of individuals. Mr. Smith added – 'remind staff that recent legislation makes them liable to prosecution if their actions help to create unsafe or unhealthy conditions at work. The law does not allow them to hide behind the management'.
3. Prepare the memo to section supervisors and managers for them to meet Mr. Smith. Include an agenda of topics and matters to be discussed.
4. Prepare suitable notices to be fixed in a prominent position in:
   (*a*) spirit room;
   (*b*) paper stores.
5. Prepare for Mr. Smith a list of those to be seen. Give brief details of faults. Give him date and times. Allow half an hour between each.

Assignment No. 19

You are the full-time secretary of the Newtown Modern Developments Ltd. Social Club. This club is for the benefit of all who work for Newtown Modern Developments. One of the Club's sub-sections is the Drama Group which is hoping to present the new play by Andrew McBacon, 'The Secret Anxiety'. You have agreed to become the business manager for the production of the play. The following are the tasks and duties involved.

1. You must write to the publishers, Drama Publications Ltd., to ask if they and the author will give the Drama Group permission to present the play.
   Usually a fee has to be paid.
   It is intended to produce the play on Thursday, May 10th, at 7.30, Friday, May 11th, at 7.30 and Saturday, May 12th at 4.30 and 7.30, at the Exhibition Hall of Newtown Civic Centre.
   Admission will be by tickets bought in advance.
2. The Exhibition Hall must be booked for the dates of the performances and for the Wednesday evening so that a full dress rehearsal may be held. The booking arrangements are with the Entertainments Officer, Newtown District Council, Town Hall, Newtown. The booking had been provisionally made by you by phone, and is to be confirmed in writing.
3. Write to Hopeshire County Printers and ask for a quotation for the printing of tickets and programmes; the latter, four sides.
4. Send in order for the tickets. You must draft contents and layout. Information – name of group, play, date and time, price.

Adult		*Child*	
	80p		40p
	£1.20		60p

(For a child, a corner to be cut off.)
Where performed.
Indicate if different tickets to be printed for each day and for each price.

5. Send in order for programmes.
   Page 1 Group. Play. Author. Dates. Price (suggest 10p).
   Page 2. Cast – in order of appearance. Names of actors. Producer and other credits. See attached sheet from producer.
   Page 3. Details of Acts/Scenes – time and location. Synopsis of play – not more than fifteen printed lines. (The producer has given you a lengthy outline and has asked you to summarise it – you must not reveal the way the play finishes.) From his notes you must work out brief details of time and setting of each Act.
   Page 4. Advertisement by your company.
   For this send a memo to the General Manager. Ask him for layout for the advertisement. At the same time tactfully suggest a management contribution to the cost of production of the play.
6. The local press must be informed. The editor should be sent a complimentary ticket and programme. He would appreciate details of the dress rehearsal so that his photographer can come along.
7. Costumes, if any, will have to be ordered. Also, you may have to order special items of furniture – on loan from a local quality furniture stores.
8. Refreshments. When booking the Exhibition Hall you must indicate that you wish to supply refreshments and state what equipment you will require. Your own Social Club Catering Committee will supply the rest.
9. The Business Manager of a play is normally responsible for keeping an account of money received and spent, and of presenting a brief financial statement to the Management Committee of the Company's Social Club.
   The following items should be considered for this: number of tickets of each type sold each day; number of programmes; receipts from sale of refreshments on each occasion. Expenditure – cost of printing – cost of hiring hall – expenditure on refreshments.

Notes from the producer, Mr. Oliver S. Johnson, to you, the Social Club Secretary, re 'The Secret Anxiety'.

This play has a cast of eight people.

John Copewell.	Lionel Manager.
Heather Copewell, his wife.	Hilary Hope.
Michael Copewell, their son.	Timothy Turnford.
Avril Copewell, their daughter.	Liz Sweeting.
Anthony Greensand.	Michael Brompton.

Alex Greensand, his father. Joseph Shortear.
Linda Greensand, his mother. Sandra Turniston.
Linda Wildbird. Susan Caterwell.

Most of the cast have suggested stage costume except Alex Greensand who needs a costume to suggest that he might have been a Naval Officer during the Second World War.

The play is set in a summer bungalow at Sandsea – the scenes are indoors. The Social Club maintenance men John Carpenter and William Gardiner will take on stage management. They will need to hire furniture to suggest an early 20th-century decor: glass-fronted, leaded cabinets; bookcases: dark oak or walnut; sideboards, dining table. A radio and gramophone (or record player) but not music centre. I suggest you write to Joiners and Carpenters, of Newtown High Street.

The Play

John and Heather Copewell are staying at their summer bungalow at Sandsea: one Friday in June. With them their son, Michael, not yet 30, and their daughter, Avril, a student at Portville Polytechnic. Avril has invited her boy friend to visit them. He is Anthony Greensand, a young engineer from Portbridge. Michael is very protective of Avril and resentful of Anthony. He decides to part them. Heather, their mother, is not keen to encourage Michael, not because she dislikes Anthony (in fact she has taken a liking to him) but because Anthony's surname recalls an unhappy relationship with a man of a similar name when she was younger. She subjects first Avril, and then Anthony when he arrives, to a barrage of cross examination, posing questions that will help to determine if Anthony's father is the Alex Greensand she once knew. Every answer confirms her fears and makes her more anxious to separate her daughter from Anthony. As time proceeds she becomes more unpleasant. As John listens to his wife's questions he becomes more and more suspicious that his wife's former relationship with this man leaves much to be desired. Heather is determined to separate the young lovers.

On the following day while Heather and John are heatedly discussing her relationship with Alex Greensand, Avril comes in and announces that she and Anthony are now engaged. She also says that Mr. and Mrs. Greensand are in the area and will be visiting them. Heather is desperate and becomes more and more panic stricken, especially as her husband seems to delight in encouraging the visit to spite her. Suddenly he turns and sees Anthony in profile and recognises in him the face of a woman he once knew and loved. 'Was your mother's name Linda Wildbird?' he asked, and when Anthony says that it was he declares that the marriage cannot go on. The mother, at first relieved that her husband has changed his mind, suddenly realises that he too is in a state of panic. The scene moves to a close to reveal that Avril's father had had a son by Linda Wildbird and that the two lovers appear to be stepbrother and sister.

The last Act opens with the arrival of Mr. Greensand while Mrs. Copewell is out of the room. Anthony loses restraint and accuses him of an affair with Avril's mother. He relates how this has emerged in the questioning. Mr. Greensand is amazed and demands to see her. When she enters she does not recognise him: although the facts fitted the description he was not the person – but it could have been his cousin.

Anthony denounces his mother, who is still not in. He repeats Mr. Copewell's confession and Mr. Greensand decides to argue it out with his wife. Mr. Copewell goes out – she comes in and is horrified at what is said. When Mr. Copewell returns he does not recognise her, but as they meet Anthony sees another woman pass the window. He calls out to her, 'Auntie Linda', and she comes in to be revealed – Linda Wildbird, the cousin of Mrs. Greensand and the woman previously in Mr. Copewell's life. The two youngsters are now free to marry.

Assignment No. 20

International Construction Supplies Ltd., of Industry Road, Newtown, has acquired additional premises from Automotive Products, which has moved to another town. The new premises are being adapted to become the new site for the Administration and Secretarial Section. The open-plan system will be in use, although areas for senior management will be so developed to make confidential meetings possible. You are the General Manager's personal secretary and he has outlined the transfer plans.

In the new building will be reception, secretarial, wages and general accounts, computer, sales, purchasing. The secretarial and accounting sections will be upstairs. The move will be spread over a week. On Saturday and Sunday – stores and equipment relating to these sections will be transferred. The reception staff will move in and prepare for other sections who may need guidance to come across – and to carry on reception duties. The telephone switchboard has been installed and will come into operation on Saturday. New telephones have been installed in the new building, allocated to staff as before. One or two new extensions. Switchboard will receive all company's calls. New building – all staff will have old extension numbers – prefixed with four. Printers to be given instruction for new directory. Sales will be in new building on Monday; Secretarial on Tuesday; Purchasing on Wednesday; Computer on Thursday; Wages and Accounts on Friday. Each of them will go through packing-up procedure in old building on previous afternoon. Managers, their Personal Secretaries and typists will go across on the Friday before anyone else moves. Generally – desk drawers to be emptied of contents and put into special boxes provided. Includes personal property. Stick label with name on desk, chair, equipment used by individual. Also on box. Add department. Department leaders to see that the name of department fixed to all other equipment and property. Persons in charge of stores and equipment to organise material for transfer on the Saturday and Sunday. Preparation of material for move to be done by 2.30 on the afternoon of the move. The company's general staff will move *all* goods to vans and put them in place. Staff will report to new building on morning of transfer. They must not shift anything. If things are not where they should be, contact supervisors, who will organise general staff to put things right. New buildings will have own car park – management at front – others in large car park at rear. All car users will be allocated a space on request (N.B. special memo on car parking). On ground floor near reception – a room for tea, coffee and very light refreshments. Main meals will still be at old building. Old building will be adapted for factory usage after move to new building. Note – computer transfer being spread over longer period. Their staff concerned already have a timetable to which they will continue to work. General date of transfer – three weeks ahead. Management – Friday, May 15th. Others follow as indicated.

1. You are to use this material to prepare a suitably organised memorandum to managers and section heads. Indicate that you are including a copy of the Planners' layout.
2. Prepare a special set of instructions for guidance of secretarial section.
3. Prepare, as a general notice
   (*a*) timetable of moves;
   (*b*) details about refreshments and meals.
4. Send memo to printer about new internal telephone directory. Assume that you are giving him a typed list of numbers.
5. Prepare memo about car parking in new block.
6. Prepare a handout for the press about the move.

Assignment No. 21

Mr. Jackson has recently returned from a conference on management techniques. Of the topics presented and discussed he found himself interested in schemes whereby staff could vary the hours during which they worked. In his notebook he entered the following points:

1. idea came from Germany, in particular from a firm in the aircraft industry;
2. staff had commuting problems;
3. basically the scheme allows people to come in when they like between certain hours and leave when they like between certain hours. A central period during the day when all are present;

4. scheme related to worker's contract arrangements;
5. some employers now using the scheme said that their staff were much happier;
6. problems of lateness and lost time seem to have disappeared;
7. surprisingly one manager said that there was very little demand for overtime;
8. because people were much happier the production was much better;
9. could be possible to organise the occasional half-day.

He circulated these notes to his colleagues to be discussed at the next staff meeting. They showed interest.

Production Manager – It sounds a good idea.
Office Supervisor: I could see trouble with recording time. I think it would be so easy to fiddle. We can't be expected to be around all the time in the morning and again in the afternoon.
Production Manager : That's easy enough. My people clock in and out already. It would simply be a matter for the people who deal with the time schedule to devise a scheme to cover everybody.
Office Supervisor: That doesn't solve the problem. At least two of my girls would get their friends to book them in.
Accounts Manager: I am afraid my men would feel clocking in beneath their dignity. I suggest we ask them to sign themselves in and out in a book.
Production Manager: Whatever the checking system I think we ought to give it a try.
Supervisor Radio Assembly Section: I like the idea, but I am wondering about the effect on production figures. Our system depends on everybody being present at the same time – at the moment for eight hours – but under this scheme for five hours if you allow for lunch.
Mr. Jackson: Perhaps we could examine the radio assembly process to see if something can be done to include your women. If they get left out they are sure to be most upset – after all they have school and shopping problems. This scheme does mean that individuals can arrange times to suit their problems.
Office Manager: What scheme do you propose?
Mr. Jackson: Everyone must be in by 10.00 a.m. No one should leave before 4.00 p.m. People can come in from 8.00 a.m. and stay on until 6.00 p.m.

Our working week is 36 hours per person. I suggest that we work in 4-week blocks – which means that 144 hours must be worked.
Production Manager: Suppose that 147 is clocked?
Mr. Jackson: What do you suggest?
Production Manager: That could be reckoned as overtime.
Accounts Manager: I think it would be better to credit it as qualifying for a complete morning or afternoon off.

Mr. Jackson: I think I would prefer that. It would be a means of satisfying the person who wants a day or half-day off – to go to Wimbledon, perhaps, during the tennis season. Alternately we could let them use it to have an extended lunch hour occasionally.

At this point, Mr. Jackson took a check and found that all were in favour of the scheme and of the hours suggested. The Production Manager still had reservations about excess hours. It was agreed to offer the scheme to the staff. Details would be sent to the Union Officials on the production side and to the Staff Association for the office and management side.

You, as Mr. Jackson's personal secretary or assistant, were present. He now wants you to draw up a memorandum about the scheme, summarising the material in his notes and additional points that had been raised at the meeting.

Distribution:
(*a*) members of staff meeting;
(*b*) Chairman of Staff Association;
(*c*) Convenor of firm's branch of the trade union to which the men belong.

Send an accompanying request to the last two that the matter be discussed and a report be made to Mr. Jackson, either in writing or by a personal meeting.

Assume that the scheme has been accepted and that all sections prefer excess time to be counted for an afternoon or morning off, or towards an extended lunch. Prepare a notice announcing the introduction and details of the scheme (clocking in/signing in as appropriate – special working arrangements are being considered for radio assembly personnel).

Assignment No. 22 (See Fig. 6.)

Road Accident — Newtown High Street — 18.11.79
On Friday, November 18th, 1979, at 12.50 p.m. John Henry Newman, Salesman, 39 Old Church Lane, Bridgewayton, age 39 (d.o.b. 5.6.38) was driving a Fiat Mirafiori 1600S (SSA 418 S) along High Street, Newtown, in a northerly direction. Employed by Bridgeway Industrial Chemists, of Bridgewayton. Also in the car:

Next to the driver – Charles Darwin, 44 Sealink Avenue, Somerton, Chemist, d.o.b. 4.7.44.
Behind driver – Miss Florence Nightingale, 217 Mayfair Crescent, Somerton, Secretary, d.o.b. 6.1.57.
Speed 20 mph – Market day.

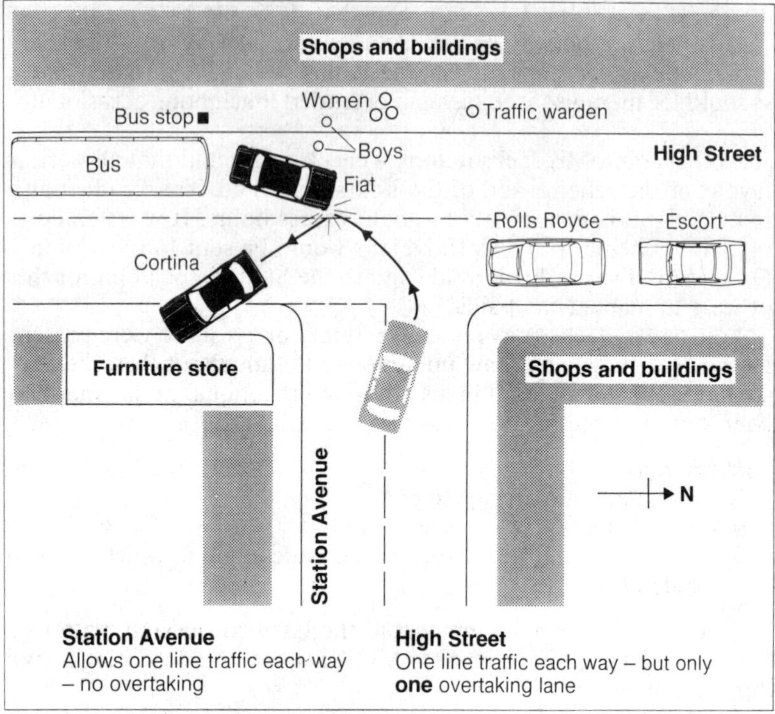

Fig. 6

On pavement three women were talking:

Mrs. Henrietta Maria Swift, 15 Windham Lane, Newtown, d.o.b. 5.6.39.
Mrs. Jane Austen, 24 Windham Lane, Newtown, d.o.b. 7.8.53.
Mrs. Anne Sophocoulos, 33 Windham Lane, Newtown, d.o.b. 6.12.54.

They were in a group facing each other. With them were two children, both boys. These two were playing and chasing each other around. Jonathan Swift (d.o.b. 3.3.70) and Nicholas Austen (4.8.70). Jonathan ran out into the road as Newman's car was approaching. Acting quickly to avoid hitting the boy, he pulled out to the right and was hit by another car.

William George Grace, Assistant Stores Manager, 29 Church Lane, Newtown, d.o.b. 6.9.52, was driving a Green Ford Cortina Saloon, 1300cc (JOO 246 C). He approached the junction of Station Avenue and High Street, driving in the centre of the road and, without stopping, turned left into the High Street, making a wide curve in doing so. He hit the Fiat and rebounded on to the pavement and went into the window of a furniture shop. Damage was also caused to items of furniture in the shop window area. Fortunately there was nobody on the pavement in this area. He received some cuts, but no serious injuries. Newman and his passengers were thrown about the car but suffered only shock. In the Cortina also was Miss Alison Price, of 47 Fox Road, Newtown, Shorthand Typist, d.o.b. 5.11.54. She also received cuts and bruises. According to a traffic warden on duty he gave no signals when turning out.

On January 8th, 1980, at Hopeshire County Sessions, Grace was convicted of:

driving without due care and attention;
having two defective front tyres;
defective brakes;
being under the influence of drink.

He received a two-year suspended sentence, and had his licence taken away for three years. Because he was driving an unroadworthy car his insurance was invalid and the Insurance Company, the Universal Car Insurance Company, declined to make any payments.

Grace would not accept full responsibility and claimed that the accident was caused by the child.

Newman, on the advice of Newtown Insurance Company, was asked to sue for damages from both the mother and Grace.

The furniture shop's insurers, World Wide Insurance, has also instructed the owners to sue, for damages, both drivers and the mother.

Witnesses:

1. Captain William Cook – 'The Arethusa', Nelson Village, near Seaport. Driving Rolls Royce, registration WHC 1 – had stopped just before the junction – driving along High Street in a southerly direction. He saw Grace pull out at speed, etc. No passenger. Age 63, d.o.b. 4.8.14.
2. Mrs. Hetty Sharpe – 46 The Heights, Newtown. Driving Escort (SSS 261 H) – no passenger. Age 38, d.o.b. 3.9.39. Driving behind Rolls. Saw women talking – saw boy run into the road.
3. Traffic Warden – Robert Painter, 8 Arden Road, Newtown. Age 45, d.o.b. 10.4.32. Facing junction and saw cars collide. Called police on intercom.
4. Bus driver. James Crankshaft. Age 51, d.o.b. 1.5.26. 46 Highbridge, Oldville. Newtown Bus Services – Route 5X, Bus registration No. JLO 441 H. Stopped at request stop – driving behind Newman.
5. Jeremy Sharpe. Passenger on bus, at front upstairs. Age 34, d.o.b. 8.10.43. 16 Wellington Villas, Newtown.

Police called to accident:
Sgt. Henry Wise, 246
PC Brian Bodington, 418
PC Alan Dickens, 663
WPC Emily Bronte, 24

All of Hopeshire County Constabulary, Newtown Division.

James Joyce, the Inspector of Claims of Newtown Motor Insurance Co., received claim from Newman. Inspected car – satisfied with roadworthiness – confirmed also by police investigation – reported damage to Fiat and authorised action for repairs. Estimate: £300 +.

Furniture Stores. Manager Stephen Carpenter. Large glass window broken, window framework (aluminium alloy material) – labour charges for repair – three piece suite severely damaged by glass, other smaller items of furniture also damaged – estimate £1,000 +.

Prepare all relevant documents required for the two actions indicated.

1. Newman's letter reporting the accident to his insurers.
2. Statements by Newman's passengers.
3. Statement by bus driver.
4. Statement by Mr. Sharpe.
5. Statements by Captain Cook and Mrs. Sharpe.
6. Report by Newtown Motor Insurance Claims Inspector.
7. Letter by Solicitor representing Newman and his Insurance Company, to Clerk of Hopeshire County Sessions for a transcript of the proceedings on January 8th, 1980, when Grace was convicted.
8. Mr. Carpenter's report to his Insurance Company of what happened and his statement of damages.

Also:

9. Write out the traffic warden's report to the Chief Superintendent, Newtown Police Division.

Assignment No. 23

Messrs. Diamond and Goldman is a company which specialises in the sale of high-class jewellery and associated products. It has a number of shops of modern design in thirty different towns and cities, with the Head Office in Oldchester, where there is also a central depot which purchases the goods that are sold in all its shops. There is a craft workshop where its own range of goods is designed, and at which it carries out repairs, adjustments and modifications to items brought to its shops.

The accounts department deals with all the financial affairs of the company, which include the purchase and sale of all goods, the payment of salaries and wages, both at Oldchester and at the various branches, the purchases, maintenance, alterations and rates in respect of all its property. The staff is under the Chief Accountant. He has two assistants, one concerned with trade income and expenditure, including VAT, the other with property accounting and wages and salaries and allied matters. The company is considering changing to computer accounting. One of the assistants is leaving and a new person is to be sought by public advertisement. Both assistants are expected to visit the branches and to be conversant with all aspects of the work. There are, in addition, a Sales and Purchasing Manager and a Property Manager.

The new person should be well qualified – have had plenty of industrial and other experience. A graduate would be very welcome. The man leaving took a keen interest in local affairs.

As the Managing Director's personal secretary, or general assistant, you are expected to make arrangements to advertise the post and send out, to those who enquire, an application form and a sheet giving general information about the company, the job and the district. You should design a suitable application form for this purpose. When you have arranged with the Managing Director the date for the interview, call the applicants for interview and, as far as the successful candidate is concerned, send her a letter to the effect that she has been selected. Ask her to confirm acceptance and send her details of starting arrangements.

Below you will find extracts from the 'Oldchester Guide to Visitors' and the Town Directory which might be used when you prepare the information sheet. You should be selective and be prepared to summarise.

Extract from the 'Oldchester Guide to Visitors'

Oldchester is the County town of Hopeshire. Its origin goes back to Roman times due to its favourable position by the Oldchester river, which rises in the Downs and flows into the English Channel at Portville. It grew as a town in the Middle Ages and received its charter from Edward I. The old part of the city is centred around the cathedral and a fine medieval guildhall. The main Cathedral Avenue leads, in one direction, to the city wall, beyond which is the famous Oldchester Castle, which is now in the care of the Department of the Environment. In the opposite direction the road leads through the East Gate to the newly developed shopping precinct, which attracts people from all over Hopeshire and the adjacent counties.

Beyond the eastern wall a very attractive modern garden suburb has developed, and on the southern outskirts of this there has developed a small industrial and trading estate where electronic goods, various electrical domestic applicances and a range of modern furniture are made. This industrial estate has easy access to the Oldchester Eastern Station on the Southern Region. The town also has good exit roads leading to the M3 and to the major trunk roads serving other parts of the county. At Portville there are facilities for travel to the Continent of Europe and a newly built container depot.

Oldchester is an ideal central spot for many interesting journeys and expeditions to the Downlands, to the Early Stone Age and Iron Age settlements, Roman villas, many fine medieval churches, cottages and inns. The river and its tributaries offer opportunities for fishing and for sailing and canoeing.

(The Guide offers more detailed information about all the places of which Oldchester is a centre and has a full section on various types of holiday accommodation.)

Extract from Oldchester Town Directory. (Copies of this are available from the Oldchester Town Hall.)

Transport

There is a fine modern bus depot near the shopping precinct. A regular service links the Town Centre with the stations, Oldchester Central and Oldchester Eastern, and with the outlying areas. A half-hourly service runs to Portville and Newtown and long-distance buses connect with other parts of England.

Schools and colleges

The Southdown Polytechnic is situated in College Avenue, not far from Central Station.

Oldchester College of Further Education provides a wide range of courses. Details can be obtained from the Principal.

Cathedral College, Cathedral Close,
Downland Upper School, Downland Rise Way.

These are private schools for children from 13 to 19.

The following schools are provided by the Hopeshire Education Authority.

Oldchester County Comprehensive.
Simon de Montfort Comprehensive.
The Archbishop's School.
Downland Junior and Primary.
Roman Junior and Primary.
Greenhills Junior and Primary.

Banking

All the major five banks have branches both in the Old Town and in the shopping precinct.

Estate Agents

Messrs. Carpenter & Boxman, Cathedral Avenue.
The Chapter House Estate Agents, Cathedral Avenue.
The New Housing Agents, Oldchester Shopping Precinct.

Entertainment

The Roman Circle Cinema.
The Civic Centre – for dancing and concerts.
The Shakespeare Theatre.
The New Bowling Alley.

Public Recreation

There are three golf courses:
The Royal Golf Club. Secretary, N. Player, Esq.
The Avenue Golf Club. Secretary, Mrs. E. Caddy.
The Southway Golf Club. Secretary, Mr. A. Best.

Facilities for cricket, football, tennis, swimming and a range of other sports and games are provided at the Oldchester Park and Public Gardens.

Note

The Company's Head Offices are at:
Pearlman Way,
Oldchester Industrial Estate,
Hopeshire.

Assignment No. 24

At an informal meeting of the staff of Stereosounds Ltd., the suggestion was made to the management that it would be a good idea if someone tried to obtain some trading concessions. It was pointed out that many other firms had been able to do this. The Personnel Officer said that he would see what could be done.

1. Compose suitable letters for him to send to:
   (*a*) National Electricals, which distributes the Company's and other people's goods. The most suitable concession would be discount.
   (*b*) The local theatre. Suggest a block of reduced price seats for performances early in the week. Point out that the company advertises the theatre's performances and other activities on all its notice-boards.
2. Write the reply – favourable – of the local theatre.

3. At the end of two weeks the Personnel Officer has received the following:
   National Electricals – 10% discount – all goods – cash only.
   Glittering Jewellers – 10% discount on cash sales. 5% discount on credit card sales.
   Firmtread Tyres – 8% discount on tyres and exhausts before VAT is charged.
   Hopeshire Football Stadium – offers 10 free tickets for each Cup or League Match.
   Local theatre – a block of 20 tickets each week for Tuesday performances – half price. Tickets will be sent to the Personnel Officer.
   Southern Car Dealers – 10% off spares pre VAT; 5% off new Cars.
   Letters have gone out to thirty others so far.
   Agreed that the firm issues cards to say that staff are employed by it. Cards are now being prepared for all staff.

   Prepare a suitable notice on the above, to be given to staff.

Assignment No. 25

John Spoke is employed as a senior motor vehicle engineer at Wonder Garages. He was asked by a friend, Richard Burbage, to examine the latter's car and give him a written report on it, to be used to help sell the vehicle. It was a Saloon Car, luxury model, 1600cc, registered six years ago. His friend bought it three years ago. In reply to his questions he assured him that he had had no trouble with it and that he had not been involved in any accident, not even a minor one.

Mr. Spoke made his examination and entered the following notes in his book:

Engine – original. Good condition. Slight oil leak. Plugs and points recently renewed. Carburettor satisfactory. Starter motor and coil both replaced. Radiator and hose – no defects. New battery. Exhaust – replaced this year.
Running quite smoothly. Gears – no problems. Clutch plate – may need renewing. Starts well.

Chassis. Suspension O.K. Steering – passed M.O.T. month ago. Brakes – front shoes will need replacing later on. Wheels* – pressure good. Good for another 5,000 miles. Spare wheel in good condition. *Balanced.

Electrical system. Can't detect faults. Lights poor. Front alignment in order. Windscreen wiper blades need to be replaced.

Body work. For six years, reasonably good. Undersealed. No noticeable damage. One or two rust spots. Near side door windows are sticking. Mileage 38,066. Regularly serviced – have seen garage receipts to confirm this. (Not this Garage.)

You are the secretary in the service station. He gave you these and asked you to set them out as a formal report – from him. You were **not** to use the firm's headed paper. The report would need details: make – colour – registration. Engine number. You were to assume that you had been given these.

About three months later the chief servicing engineer at Worldwide Motors, also of the same town, contacted John Spoke to ask him if Burbage had been correct when he said he had not been in an accident. He explained that the person who bought the car had been having trouble and that one or two defects on the near side of the car, including a metal fracture beneath the driver's passenger's door, suggested that he had been involved in an accident. The repair costs for it would be expensive.

John Spoke decided that this could be serious and asked you to write to his friend, outlining the information he had received. The friend was to be asked to confirm in writing what he had previously said.

In reply, Burbage recalled an episode which had occured a year before on holiday, which he had forgotten. Compose this letter.

On behalf of Mr. Spoke, write to Burbage to tell him that you will have to inform Worldwide Motors. Also write to the latter, enclosing a copy of Burbage's letter.

Finally, the new owner, Mr. J. Spratt, having received the news and being advised by Worldwide Motors, wrote to Mr. Burbage to claim the cost of the work resulting from this accident. He pointed out that the car had been bought in good faith, believing that there had been no accident. Compose this letter.

Assignment No. 26

On February 2nd, 1980, Mr. Jonathan Jones, of 9 Chelmsford Close, Newtown, called at the Newtown branch of the Citizens Advice Bureau concerning problems he had been having about a music centre that he had purchased. The officer on duty, Mrs. Agnes Judge, made the following notes:

Mr. Jonathan Jones, 9 Chelmsford Close. 2.2.80.
Electronic Supplies, 10 High Street, N.T. Oct.4/79. Paid £175 cash for music centre complete – radio/control unit, 2 speakers, 1 record player. 1 wk. delivery. 18/10 phoned E.S.S. – out of stock – due in promise 1 wk. 1/11 – still undelivered. Wrote to E.S.S. Head Office, London. 10/11 second letter to Head Office. 18/11 – third letter – demanded money back (with interest) – stated copy being sent to solicitor asking him to act. 22/11 – delivered. Installed. Spkrs – no sound. Rec. Player (*a*) automatic starting not working; (*b*) 3 speed – only 78rpm. 22/11 phoned. Would collect 23/11. Not collected. Phone 0900 24/11 – E.S.S. forgot. Collected 11.00 a.m. that day. Receipt

left. 25/11 rang to enquire – no trace of anything. Would look. 25/11 E.S.S. called to collect! Further phone call – would enquire. 27/11 phone call recd – traced to Oldbridge – being returned to Newtown 29/11. 30/11 letter received. Spkrs + player being sent to manufacturers suppliers (Mikardo Supplies and Maintenance) for check. 7/12 wrote to E.S.S. to enquire. No reply. 11/12 another letter – still no reply. Phoned 13/12 – letters not received – Xmas to blame. Would check.
15/12 postcard received. Letters acknowledged. 'Receiving attention'. 18/12 have written to manufacturers. No promise of a reply before Xmas. E.S.S. – closing 23/12 to 2/1 incl. 2/1 no correspondence. Phoned. Asked manuf. suppliers' address – E.S.S. would send it. 4/1 letter from E.S.S. Cannot give address. Against H.O. policy – but promised to follow up.
7/1 wrote to H.O.
9/1 H.O. acknowledged – would follow up.
9/1 H.O. asks Newtown for summary of correspondence with Jones. Received 10/1 Telex to manufacturers suppliers.
10/1 manufacturers suppliers reply to Telex – will send replacements.
1/2 still no parts. Jones visits C.A.B.

Use the material supplied above.

1. Prepare the summary of correspondence referred to above.
2. Prepare Telex message and reply.
3. From this material compose suitably worded letters to be sent to both manufacturers suppliers and Electronics Super Supplies (Head Office).
4. Head Office sends apology – replacements the following day – to Mr. Jones.
5. Finally Mr. Jones is happy. Prepare his letter of thanks to C.A.B.

Assignment No. 27

John Brightman and Miss Helen Troy, who are engaged to be married, have decided to make all the arrangements for the wedding. The event itself has been fixed for Saturday, June 21st, 1980. Because she is a private secretary, Helen finds herself doing most of the work. The couple agree on the names of eighty guests, in addition to members of their immediate family, to whom formal invitations will be sent.

Miss Troy lives in Portville, at 'Arethusa', 100 Admiral Drive, the home of her parents, Dr. Michael Robert and Mrs. Deborah Troy, both of whom are abroad but will be back two weeks before the wedding. Her two younger sisters, Greta and Kirsten, are to be bridesmaids. The younger of her two brothers, Richard, will be a page boy. The older brother, Bernard, about eighteen months younger than

Helen, will be at the ceremony and reception, although at present working in France.

John Brightman is the son of James Henry and Elizabeth Brightman, of Sandville. His older brother, Philip, will be acting as best man, and will be accompanied by his wife, Jane.

The ceremony will take place at Portville parish church of St. Michael and All Angels at 3.00 p.m. The Rural Dean of Portville, the Rev. John Upright, who is also Vicar of St. Michael's, will officiate.

The church is quite close to the Mariner Hotel, at which the reception is to be held. Helen writes to the Manager to say that she and John would like a formal meal. He replies that the Trafalgar Room is ideal for the purpose. Waiter service will be provided. Two menus are available, details of which are included in his reply. The room is available from 5.00 p.m. After dinner the tables can be moved and the room made ready for the dance. The cost for the dinner would be £10.00 per head, exclusive of wines. The hotel's resident band, The Northern Lights, would be available at a fee of £125. The manager would agree, if the couple wished, to engage a band of their own choice.

Helen's reply accepts the Trafalgar Room and the band suggested. She will inform the manager of the number requiring each of the menus about a week before the ceremony. An aunt has offered to make the wedding cake. Helen would like the cutting of this to be done at the end of the formal dinner. She says that John will arrange with the manager concerning the supply of drinks during the evening.

She writes to two photographers to ask for an estimate for wedding photographs – Real Life Studios and John Shooter Pictures. Decides on former – asks for pictures at the church, home and reception. She understands that proofs will be available by 9.00 p.m.

About two weeks before the wedding she writes to the editor of the 'Portville Echo and Gazette' to give him details about the arrangements.

To be done

1. Using the information given above, prepare Helen's formal invitation to her guests. It should be in accordance with conventional practice.
2. Prepare the letter that will go with it to give details of the reception dinner. Submit two different menus appropriate to the occasion. In the letter ask guests to indicate choice of menu when they reply to the invitation.
3. Prepare the correspondence between Helen and the Manager.
4. Prepare Helen's letter to the photographers requesting an estimate and her letter of acceptance in reply to the first photographer.
5. Write out the notice that will appear in the 'Portville Echo and Gazette' after the wedding has taken place.

6. The Portville and District Youth Council is planning a series of leaflets for young people. These are under the general heading, 'Can We Help You?' The Secretary has asked Helen and John to prepare one on the practical problems of getting married. Prepare this leaflet – use the material given above and any other information that you can obtain. The following suggestions might be followed:
   (*a*) what do I have to do to get married? – Where? (church – chapel – registry office). Check procedure.
   (*b*) Dress.
   (*c*) The reception; the cake.
   (*d*) The pictures.
   (*e*) The honeymoon.
   (*f*) Final page – what it costs.

Assignment No. 28

For the purposes of the European parliamentary election, Britain has been divided into a number of Euro-constituencies, each comprising a number of British parliamentary constituencies. For the South Hopeshire Euro-constituency ten such local constituencies have been brought together. Newtown has been designated as the administrative centre for electoral purposes.

At its last annual conference the United Europe Party agreed that it would contest all the constituencies and recommended the formation of Euro-councils for the purpose. These were to have the same boundaries as the Euro-constituencies. The South Hopeshire United Europe Party Euro-council consists of the Chairman, Secretary and Treasurer of each local party association together with one elected representative for every two hundred paid-up members. This council is to be appointed biennially.

Nationally it has been agreed that each local association should pay to the Euro-council a contribution of 50p per member, additional to any other subscriptions.

You were appointed Secretary of the Hopeshire Euro-council when it was formed in 1978. It is now time for the local associations to designate their members for the period 1980–2, prior to the holding of the 1980 Annual General Meeting. In connection with this you should:

1. Devise a form to be sent to each local association to seek details of their representatives. The largest constituency, according to the last membership returns, had 1,179 members. When you know the membership you will expect to send notices of meetings and other business direct to their home addresses.
2. Prepare a letter to accompany this. In it you should give a date by which the form is to be returned – set a minimum of four weeks

from the date of the 1980 A.G.M. – Friday, April 25th. If you do not get the form back in time, representatives may not get details of the A.G.M. before April 25th. You should also give advance notice of the date of the A.G.M. The person to whom your letter is sent should be reminded that the 1980 contributions are due and that the Euro-council treasurer is waiting to receive them.

3. Prepare the notice of meeting and agenda for A.G.M. It will be held in the Newtown Town Hall Council Chamber. In addition to the minutes of the previous A.G.M. the council will receive reports from the Chairman and Treasurer, will appoint the officers – Chairman, Vice-Chairman, Secretary, Treasurer – and the executive committee, consisting of nine members.

   Members of the Portville Association have submitted a motion for discussion: 'The South Hopeshire Euro-Council views with concern the serious effect that the policy of the E.E.C. is having on the nation's fishing industry. It views with alarm the rapid increase in prices for fish and the large number of fishermen unemployed. It calls upon the British representatives in the Euro-Parliament to raise the matter and press for action.' It will be proposed by the Chairman of Portville Association, Captain L. J. George R.N. (ret.), and seconded by the Secretary of the Sandsea Association, Mr. S. S. Fishman.

   N.B. Nominations for the officers and executive committee must be received by Saturday, April 11th.

   After the formal business has ended, the A.G.M. will be addressed by the party's national president, who is also an elected representative to the Euro-Parliament. He is Sir Andrew McSteven.

   You will be enclosing the following: a duplicated copy of the minutes of the last A.G.M., and a duplicated copy of the statement of accounts for the year ending December 31st, 1979. For this assignment you do not have to prepare them.

Assignment No. 29

Reference should be made to Assignment No. 28.

At the Annual General Meeting of the South Hopeshire United Europe Party Euro-council, you, as Secretary, made the following notes:

Present: Chairman (Noel Speakerman, J.P.). 110 others plus Sec. & Treas. (Names in attendance book.)

Minutes – mtg. at Portville Cty. Comprehensive School, Fri. 27/4/79. Amendment: Miss Elizabeth Wrighton, not Lionel Lloyd, nominated Lord Jenkinson to exec. cttee.

Arising: 1. Change in Britain driving on left to driving on right. Chmn. raised with leader of Brit. European Parlt. Group. Enquiries showed suggestion was made at public meeting in France by prominent figure there. No formal proposals. Brit. leader said any such proposals would be strongly resisted. 2. Proposals for Political Union. Said I had written to all other party associations in S. Hopes. re motion pol. union. All replied – no support.

Chmn's Report. (1) Growth in membership – all 10 associations – now over 18,000. (2) All assocns but one had raised contribution quota. (3) Exec. cttee. 10 meetings – it raised with party's reps. in Euro-Parlt. and at Westminster the following matters: farm prices – butter shortage in Brit. and sale of surplus out of Europe – growing size of continental lorries – proposals to simplify customs procedures – possibility of legislation to control multi-nationals in E.E.C. – differences in trade union legislation within E.E.C. (4) Small committee to explore possibilities of H.Q. in S. Hopeshire for Party's Euro-council. Possible sites – Newtown, Portville, Oldchester Memorandum to local assoc's October. (5) Future – plans being considered for next Euro-Parlt. elections. Will need a prospective candidate.

Discussion on above – contributions too high – do we need H.Q.? Motion re simplified customs. 'The S.H. Unit. Europ. Party Euro-council believes that urgent attention should be given by the U.K. Govt. and by Brit. members of Euro-Parlt. to proposals to simplify customs rules and procedures within EEC'. Proposed by Mr. J. Watt. Seconded Lady Lakeston. Unanimous. Instruction – send motion to Chanc. of Excheq. & Prime Minister – to Chairman Europ. Council of Ministers – all Brit. members of Euro. Parlt. Chairman's report adopted.

Treasurer – accts. and balance sheet circulated. Audited. Gave brief explanation. No questions. Report adopted.

Appointments. Ch'mn. temp vacated chair. V/ch'mn – said ch'mn eligible for further term. From chair proposed re-apptmt of Noel Speakerman J.P. as ch'man. Unam. agreed. Mr. Speakerman returned to chair. V/Ch'mn. Mr. Lukins not standing again. 4 noms. 1st count Mr. J. Watt 47, Mr. R. Stevenson 12, Mr. G. Shaw 18. Lady Lakeston 35. 2nd count with trans votes. Mr. J. Watt 55, Lady Lakeston 53. J. Watt Elected.

Sec. & Treas. Both eligible. No other nomin. Both declared elected. Exec. Cttee. Miss M. Anders; Ms. Elspeth Bonview; Col. S. Jeffreys; Lord Jenkinson; Lady Lakeston; Rev. S. McBride; Mr. G. Shaw; Mr. R. Stevenson (Mr. J. Watt had been nominated – now ex officio). Chairman asked for further nominations – Capt. George prop. by S. S. Fishman: Sec. by L. Stevens. No others. All 9 apptd.

Portville motion – (Agenda). Capt. George prop. Each year Britain allowed 5% less of home waters catch – now down to 25%. Home-caught fish prices up 150% in two yrs. Imported fish from Far East – even dearer. Intensive fishing exhausting home waters shoals. Fish moving out into Atlantic – need to overhaul boats – many useless for Atlantic. Urged need for radical review of policy. S. S. Fishman – took up with effect on British canning industry in decline. A further blow to boat construction industry. Support by many speakers. Col. Jeffreys felt blame should be put on Brit. Govt. He said Govt. was more concerned with industrial advantages than with fishing or agriculture. Motion accepted unam.

Further proposed that motion be sent to British members of Europ. Parlt. – to Europe Council of Ministers – to English minister responsible for fishing industry.

Next years AGM – Fri. 24/4 – Oldchester.

After meeting closed – Sir Andrew McSteven – 'The Future in Europe'.

1. Using this material compile the Minutes of the A.G.M.
2. A copy has to be sent to the national headquarters of the United Europe Party. Write the accompanying letter.
3. Prepare any correspondence necessary to carry out the instructions of the meeting.

Assignment No. 30

Captain Lawrence has decided to buy a house known as Chaucer Cottage, situated on the Oldchester Road, just outside Normantown, in Hopeshire. It will cost him £56,000. His own house, at 41 Burns Avenue, Newtown, is being advertised at £65,000. It is a spacious, detached bungalow in a pleasant, residential part of Newtown.

Mr. and Mrs. Broome inspected the bungalow and, after seeing the surveyor's report, decided to purchase it subject to their being able to get a mortgage. In the meantime, Captain Lawrence learns that the person selling Chaucer Cottage is emigrating and wants to complete the transaction very quickly. The date of May 31st has been given. Mr. and Mrs. Broome, however, will be unable to settle before June 30th. An accountant friend of Capt. Lawrence advises him to apply to his bank for a bridging loan. He phones the manager of his local bank, Mr. S. Cash, who asks him to call. The manager discusses the problem and explains the procedure.

A form of application for the loan has to be completed and submitted. If the loan is granted, the bank manager will pay the £56,000 and other costs direct to the estate agents acting for owner of Chaucer Cottage. Captain Lawrence will also be asked to sign a form authorising his own estate agent, Higher and Higher, of High Street, Newtown, to pay direct to the bank all money received from the sale of the bungalow. The estate agent will be asked to deduct any legal fees and other legitimate expenses. When the money has been received, Mr. Cash will deduct the amount of the loan and interest that has accrued and pay any balance into Captain Lawrence's account. All details of these transactions will be recorded in the statement that Captain Lawrence usually receives.

1. Design a suitable application form for the bridging loan. It should include the normal personal details. An applicant will be expected to give information about his financial affairs – source of income, property owned and details of outstanding loans and credit cards. He will also be expected to give this information in respect of his wife. The amount of loan required should be stated. One section of the form should provide sufficient space to enable the applicant to explain carefully why he/she requires such a loan.
2. Write out the answer of Captain Lawrence to the request that he explains why he wants the loan.
3. Prepare a suitable form of instruction to the estate agent to authorise him to pay the proceeds of the sale direct to the bank.

Assignment No. 31

Following a suggestion from a member of the factory staff, the management of Newtown Computer and Electronic Machines Ltd. has decided to arrange for an open day on the second Saturday in July. The company has set aside for the purpose a large restaurant and an assembly room leading from it. The aim of the open day is:

1. to enable residents of Newtown to find out about the above company's activities;
2. to give an opportunity to prospective school and college leavers to find out about employment prospects; and
3. to provide a trade exhibition for the benefit of potential customers.

The management hopes to assemble a suitable display of the company's products, models, charts and diagrams illustrating production techniques, and pamphlets to be taken away.

It has been decided to associate the company with the Hopeshire County Appeal to provide local hospitals – in this case Newtown Fleming Hospital – with equipment and machinery which the National Health Service cannot purchase. To this end their grounds will be used on the same day for a Garden Fete, which the Company Social Club will organise.

The Publicity Officer has been given overall responsibility. As his secretary you are asked to help in preparing the following:

(*a*) A memorandum to all sections in the firm. Outline scheme. Invite two representatives from each section to serve on co-ordinating committee. Ask sections to consider their contribution to exhibition and to prepare material for a brochure or leaflet. (Publicity to do all printing, posters and display.) You want a separate statement on opportunity for school leavers. Can public visit their sections? Any problems in this – security – commercial secrets – safety regulations. Who will be responsible for section's contribution? Volunteers wanted to deal with queries. Company photographer to produce postcards for sale – HAVE SECTIONS ANY INTERESTING MATERIAL?

Garden Fete. Social Club Secretary will organise. She would like a small committee to help.

(*b*) Prepare a suitable leaflet or notice to be sent to Youth Employment and Careers Advisers, to Job Centres and to local schools and college careers teachers and lecturers. The purpose of this leaflet is to advertise open day, not deal with job opportunities.
(*c*) Prepare a notice for the Social Club Secretary, inviting the help of employees with the Garden Fete – sideshows and refreshments. She wants ideas for a three-hour arena display.
(*d*) Prepare a suitable handout for the local press.

Assignment No. 32

The Chairman of Newtown Electronics Company received the letter printed on page 128.

1. You, as Sir Alan's personal secretary, are asked to prepare for him a letter of reply. You have made these notes – acknowledge – honoured by invitation – Board to consider. Don't forget correct etiquette – check reference books.
2. He asks you to do two other letters, one to the Prime Minister and the other to the Minister for Trade and Industry. Newtown Electronics R&D unit is involved in Secret Work for the U.K. Government. As Ruritania is a foreign power the request must be referred to the P.M. and to the Department involved. Send copy of original. Invite their comments and advice. Indicate the nature of the reply sent (or enclose a copy).

Sir Alan received the reply from the Prime Minister printed on page 129.

After receiving the Prime Minister's reply, Sir Alan decided to call a special meeting of the directors of the company and asked you to attend to make a verbatim report which is given on pages 128–31.

3. Prepare the notice/letter inviting the directors to the meeting on June 16th in the company's Boardroom. The purpose is to discuss a letter from a foreign diplomat.
4. Sir Alan has asked you to summarise the discussion at the Board meeting. Do this and send a copy to each director. He also wishes you to send a copy to the Prime Minister and Alex Poster. In each

The Republic of Ruritania

The Embassy,
London,

June 1st, 1980

Sir Alan P. Dunnett, F.R.S.,
Chairman,
Newtown Electronics Co. Ltd.,
Princes Way,
Newtown,
Hopeshire.

Dear Sir Alan,

I am commanded by His Excellency, Dr. M. Leblanc, the President of the Republic of Ruritania, to inform you that he and his wife, together with representatives of the government of the Republic, intend to visit the United Kingdom in 1981.

His Excellency has expressed a wish to visit some of Britain's modern industrial companies and has specifically mentioned Newtown Electronics Company. He would be most interested in being given the opportunity to visit your Research and Development Unit which, you will know, has been favourably mentioned in the leading scientific journals.

I should be very grateful to receive your comments and to learn of any proposed arrangements.

I have the honour to be,
Yours sincerely,
Leopold von Beinum
Ambassador.

case prepare a covering letter, which should be marked 'Very Confidential'.

Transcription of discussion at Directors Meeting on June 16th

Sir Alan Dunnett: Gentlemen, thank you for coming. I have had a letter from the Ambassador of Ruritania. (He reads letter.) As soon as I received it my Secretary, on my instructions, drafted the reply (which he reads). In view of the nature of our work and of the close relations we have with the Government I decided at once to communicate the contents of both letters to the Prime Minister and the Minister at the Department of Trade and Industry. After the two had met the Prime Minister sent this reply (reads P.M.'s reply).

10 Downing Street,
Westminster, S.W.1.

June 8th, 1980

Sir Alan P. Dunnett, F.R.S.,
Chairman,
Newtown Electronics Co. Ltd.,
Princes Way,
Newtown,
Hopeshire.

Dear Alan,

Proposed Visit of President of Ruritania

I am most grateful to you for sending me a copy of the ambassador's letter.

As soon as he received his copy of your letter, Alex. Poster, the Minister at the Department of Trade and Industry, came across to me to discuss its implications.

We were most surprised that you should have received the letter, especially as we have had no indication of a proposed visit. I have consulted the Secretary to the Cabinet who assures me that, to the best of his knowledge, the Leader of the Opposition had received no communications on this matter when he was Prime Minister.

We are very concerned that the President wishes to visit your Research and Development Unit. I trust that I may take it for granted that no visiting delegation from abroad would be permitted to visit those sections involved with Government work of a confidential or secret nature. It would make me happier if you would arrange to keep me fully informed of all action that is taken in this matter.

You will realise that a visit of this nature could be politically difficult.

Yours sincerely,
Oliver Cromaparte,
Prime Minister.

From a political standpoint, the Prime Minister is rightly concerned about the matter.

I would say first of all that I feel honoured that the Ruritanians have selected us for a visit which could pave the way for an expansion of our trade with that country. On the commercial side, Ruritania needs many of our products. The developments that have been made in the field of micro-transistors are of great significance.

Great progress has been made in the production of computerised equipment to meet the needs of small companies and organisations. The Ruritanian tourist and hotel trade would be most interested in our models which enable the whole process of preparing and cooking meals to be controlled electronically. These are a few of the examples of commercial developments which would enable us to benefit from the visit.

As our correspondence with the Prime Minister shows there is another side to our work – highly secret and highly confidential – of which you all are aware, but to elaborate which would be most unwise, even at this meeting.

A major problem will be how to exclude our visitors from sections where government work is in progress without giving offence.

Michael Compson. It would be wonderful if we could break into the Ruritanian market. It would certainly send the value of our shares up.

Alan Reddingbourne. I agree, but I am equally concerned about the security risk. I don't think we should trust the Ruritanians. Their aggressive aims are well known to everybody. I think they study our know-how, develop it themselves and forget us. You know they have little respect for patent rights.

Tom Copperson. – or anybody else's rights. We shall have to be careful. If our workers hear about this they will soon start to organise industrial action to stop it – and you know what that means.

Sir Alan. Gentlemen, I think we ought to remember that this discussion is very confidential.

Brian Thickerstick. I don't accept that. I have been elected to the Board to represent the workforce. They must be told what is happening.

Sir Alan. On no account must anybody outside this room get to know what is happening.

Brian Thickerstick. The letter from the Ambassador was not marked confidential. You represent the shareholders – they will have to know. You have told the government. I represent the workers and they also have a right to know. If we don't tell them as a Board, then I shall. The Ruritanians are putting their workers into prison. I don't see why we should back their government by helping to increase their wealth because we want bigger profits.

Michael Compson. Brian, you are on the Board to represent the workers and also to consider the best interests of Newtown Electronics. I think you ought to keep politics out of it. We must trust Sir Alan to protect the national interest as far as secrets are concerned and back him up when he tries to further this firm's best interests.

Sir Alan. I would point out that no decision has been made. I certainly agree that it would be very beneficial to us if we could establish a sound commercial relationship with that country. Brian, I hope you will not rush into action that will make life troublesome for us all.

Brian Thickerstick. I accept that the Board must look after the firm's interests – but I cannot agree to proposals that are morally wrong.

David Weekson. If we make a mess of this the firm could suffer. This would mean that some of your men could lose their jobs. They won't thank you for that, Brian.

Sir Alan. I suggest that we leave this issue for now and get back to the letters.

Michael Compson. I propose that Sir Alan writes to the Ambassador to say that we are interested in the suggested visit but can make no definite arrangements until we have firm dates on which to work. This will give time for the Prime Minister to take up the question of a delegation visiting the U.K.

David Weekson. I second that.

Everybody, except Brian Thickerstick, gave their assent.

Brian Thickerstick. Will you record me as voting against?

Sir Alan (to his secretary). Will you make a note of that? I would like to suggest a small committee to look after this. Michael Compson, David Weekson and Tom Copperson agreed to serve. Brian Thickerstick refused to take part.

Sir Alan. In view of Brian's attitude I shall have to call the staff liaison committee to explain the situation to them.

The House of Commons,
S.W.1.

June 18th, 1980

Dear Sir Alan,

I was very concerned to hear from Mr. Brian Thickerstick, one of the directors of Newtown Electronics, that the company is proposing to entertain a delegation from Ruritania. As the company is involved in contract and research work for the government I find this information to be quite disturbing.

Ruritania is under criticism for its failure to respect human rights. It is well known that it does not tolerate the trade union movement.

I intend to raise the matter at question time in the House early next week. In the meantime I should be pleased to have your observations.

Yours sincerely,
Trevor Tristram
(Member for Newtown.)

On the following day Brian Thickerstick was still feeling so concerned about the matter that he wrote a letter to the M.P. for Newtown, a member of the Opposition. The latter wrote to Sir Alan Dunnett (see letter on page 131).

5. Draft a reply to this for Sir Alan. The M.P.'s letter is a misrepresentation of what has taken place. Sir Alan has asked you to produce a summary of the correspondence on the matter, to be sent to Mr. Tristram with the letter. A copy will be sent to the Prime Minister.

Assignment No 33

Mrs. Suzanne Moore has offered to make the wedding and bridesmaid's dresses for her niece, Miss Virginia Staywell, who has decided that hers will be full length and made of white satin. They bought a very expensive pattern after Virginia had been assured that it is the only one of its kind. It cost £2.25. Finally, they bought 6 metres of white satin, 1.5 metres wide at £4.50 per metre.

Having prepared the pieces of the pattern and fixed them to the satin, Mrs. Moore began the process of cutting out. With the material in place on her table she put one hand firmly on the material while she cut each piece out. Later, when she had removed the pattern paper she was horrified to find the words, such as **skirt, bottom, waist,** had been firmly and clearly impressed on the material.

She examined the pattern and found that these words had been printed with an ink very similar to that used on carbon paper – on the underside of the pattern. She took a piece of waste material to test for cleaning after she had imprinted some of the words on it but found the methods to which she was accustomed were of no use.

Having collected the pattern pieces together she took them to 'The Modern Seamstress', of the High Street, Oldville, where she had bought them and there she told her story.

'That was a stupid thing to do to put your hand over the letters on the pattern paper', replied the manageress, who decided that she could do nothing about it.

Mrs. Moore wrote a letter to the maker of the pattern, Unique Quality Patterns, Holiton. In reply, they expressed surprise and asked her to send the pattern. She decided, on advice, to send one piece. She had a letter back from the makers who admitted that the wrong ink had been used, but suggested that Mrs. Moore should have tried it out on some old material first. They sent her a cheque for the cost of the pattern.

She was most concerned, as the date of the wedding was getting nearer. She and her niece had to agree on another pattern and different material. In the meantime she wrote to the Hopeshire Consumer Association. They asked her to send to them the receipt and later wrote to the makers of the pattern and to 'The Modern Seamstress'. To the latter they pointed out that as the supplier of the pattern they were liable for the damage it had caused. The Association suggested that the makers should refund the cost of the material as well and indicated that it was prepared to back court action against the shop. It suggested that the shop might have a case against the maker.

After some consideration the pattern maker wrote to the Consumer Association to say that it accepted full responsibility and would reimburse Mrs. Moore for the cost of the white satin. It sent her a letter and a cheque which arrived a week before the wedding.

Prepare the correspondence written between Mrs. Moore and Unique Quality Patterns, between the Consumer Association and Unique Quality Patterns, and between the Consumer Association and 'The Modern Seamstress'.

Assignment No. 34

The National Universities and Higher Education Broadcasting Council is responsible for televised broadcasting on the fifth channel. It operates through a number of regional centres, one of which is the South East Area, known popularly as SEAR Television.

Professor J. Trumper, SEAR's adviser in Social Studies, has been consulting lecturers, teachers and students interested in various aspects of his work and has decided that it would be a sound idea to present a programme comparing and contrasting educational, cultural and leisure opportunities available to young people at different times in the 20th century. His idea is to explore these opportunities in a particular area, for instance, a very large youth centre, and collect as much information as possible.

He phoned the Features Editor at SEAR, Alan Soundworthy, and outlined his plans. The latter thought it was a good idea and invited Professor Trumper to send him a memorandum detailing his proposals.

The Professor wrote down his ideas and asked you, his secretary, to prepare the memorandum for him. These were his notes:

Prepare memorandum and a covering letter. Title – Education, Culture, Leisure for Young People in 20th Century. To be a comparative study of opportunities for Young People at different times – 1962–5, present youngsters born: 1933–45 – their parents born: 1925 and earlier – their grandparents born. Large numbers of young people at Youth Centres – suggest we work at one of these. Newingham Leisure and Youth Centre – 300 members 14–20. Boys and Girls. Centre caters for older and younger. Distribute questionnaire to seek relevant information about each of groups above. Follow by interview – talk about background. Letter can be backed by film. Questionnaire information to be presented – verbal summary-chart. Programme could be part of schools series – title 'Life – Now and Then'. Equally useful for Open University – 'Trends in Society'.

He has also given you a separate sheet of notes with the request, 'Would you produce a questionnaire for me?' It can be sent as an appendix to the memorandum.

To be completed by all members over 14 – not 20. Names not wanted – suggest leaders sign each. Give Sex. Age. Date of Birth. Where living (town only). Where born (town: if abroad, give country). School – M. F. Co-ed. Private/State. List types attended. Nursery (under 5). Primary. Secondary (Comprehensive, Sixth Form College). For Private. Preparatory (under 18). – post 13. Day or Boarding. Activities at Leisure Centre – Youth Centre – Badminton Club – Table Tennis Club : Youth Orchestra: Youth Drama: Youth Workshop. Activities elsewhere: Scout/Guide – Newingham Football (Youth) – Long Lane Disco Centre. Newingham Equestrians: The Ramblers: Motor Cycle Club. Space for any others.
Do not ask for activities when under 14.
Space for comments on opportunities provided.

Separate sections

(i) Parents (ii) Grandparents.
Present age (if known). Where born.
Education – Schools M. F. Co-ed.: Private – State.
If private – preparatory – over 13. Day or Boarding.
State: Grammar/Modern/Technical. If appropriate – Elementary or Secondary or Central
Age on leaving school.
Ask that activities be written down – e.g. Scouts; Guides; Brigade; Club – give details of any special activities that were organised.
Prepare this questionnaire so that sections for parents and grandparents may be taken home and completed.

Assignment No. 35

See Assignment No. 34.

Sir Alan Soundworthy, SEAR's Features Editor, was impressed by Professor Trumper's memorandum and asked Joan Prober to take charge of the Research and Production team to turn the professor's ideas into a suitable programme. She called a team conference – herself, the professor, Alec Whyman, who would deal with the research side, Tom Flash and Norman Sharpe, the cameramen, and Edmund Masterman, a specialist in educational history. You, her secretary, Alison, are also present.

The following is a transcript of their first meeting which you have taken.

Joan: We have all been introduced. Alan Soundworthy has circulated copies of the Professor's memorandum and questionnaire. I think it would be a good idea if the Professor told us more about his ideas.

Professor: Certainly. You may recall that we did a series last year on the Health Service in which we outlined the evolution of that service and asked about its future. It was successful and, as SEAR's adviser in Social Studies, I have had many letters and phone calls suggesting that we do a series in another social field. The one most popular is education and leisure.

Joan: So you see this as a series?

Professor: Yes. We could explore education – by looking at the organisation and institutions and following up with a study of recreational, leisure and cultural organisations.

Joan: Have you any ideas about the programmes?

Professor: In one of the letters I received a teacher from a coastal town told of a pupil's complaint that he was always being told by his parents and grandparents how well off he was when comparisons were made. At the same time their achievements always appeared to be much better. Our study could be focused at three points in time – that of the young people, that of the time when their parents were children and, finally, that when their grandparents were children. By selecting a large youth centre we could collect much useful information to make possible a comparison and an estimate of the progress made. The questionnaire would help to turn the information into a statistical form which would be more useful and could be related to figures from the Department of Education.

Edmund: This sounds interesting but one can overdo the use of figures. History is concerned with human beings – real men and women who have actually lived and died. We should try to humanise the programme.

Alec: There must be a balance of figures and facts on the one hand and the human interest on the other.

Joan: Alec, what do you suggest?

Alec: When the Professor's questionnaires have been returned and converted into statistical tables, Michael Jones can be asked to present these in one of the interesting chart forms through which he has built up a reputation for himself. These charts would form the basis of any discussion.

Edmund: Let us first look at the educational organisation and institutions. We could produce a series on Nursery and Infant Education, Primary, Secondary, Further and Higher Education. This would give us six programmes. Next, we could look at the Youth Service, Libraries and Museums, Music and Drama, and Sport. It might be possible to do the Administration of Leisure.

Joan: Good. That will give Alec and his research team plenty to investigate.

Tom: Can we come back to that teacher's letter. If we could get all three generations together to share experiences it would bring some life into the series.

Joan: What have you got in mind?

Tom: Let us start at Newingham. I believe they have had built an interesting theatre, in which they are producing and making drama of a high level of competence. Can we assemble there about twenty typical composite families – the younger generation, including brothers and sisters and covering, if possible, the full age range of older primary, secondary and further education or university, the parents of such a family, and the grandparents. If we can get both sets of grandparents so much the better. The catchment area of Newingham is such that we would have an interesting assortment of social types. When Alec has completed his background research we ought to have an interesting set of audience questions, the response to which would provide useful information and a very lively discussion.

Norman: The preliminary discussions at Newingham ought to lead us to some useful outside locations – one of these prison-like schools built at the end of the nineteenth century, one of the early red-brick secondary schools, a modern expensive glass built school. Again, there are places like Brownsea Island with its early Scouting connections.

Tom: The BBC and National Film Institute have some useful material – the Duke of York youth camps, the activities of the Outward Bound movement or the Duke of Edinburgh Award Scheme. Nor should we forget some of those very early school photographs which parents still treasure.

Joan: Well, Professor, we seem to be interested in your ideas. We must now do some research and produce an outline scheme. I shall suggest that we produce the series. Alec, will you, the Professor and Edmund meet together to do the research? Tom and Norman, I shall ask Alan to allocate you to me for this series. Would you both arrange to go to Newingham to do some preliminary external work at the Leisure Centre and in the town itself? Alison, my secretary, will be at everybody's disposal for any secretarial work. She will organise any typing, printing or duplicating that has to be done. I suggest we meet again a week from today. Thank you for coming.

After this meeting, Mrs. Prober has given you the following instructions which you should carry out.

1. Produce, for circulation in memorandum form, a summary of the meeting recorded above. Copies are to go to the Features Editor, to the Head of SEAR's technical services and to each of those present.
2. In the covering letter that will go to the Feature's Editor, Mrs.

Prober wishes you to include a request to produce the series.

3. Whenever the Feature's Editor is asked to approve proposals for a programme he expects to receive a short statement about the programme (its aims, scope and contents), to be passed on by him to the Director of Programmes, SEAR. Mrs. Prober wants you, using all the material you have had so far, to draft the statement and enclose it, when signed, with the memorandum and letter mentioned above.
4. Prepare for signature a letter to the County Education Officer, Hopeshire County Council, Newtown. In it you should refer briefly to the scheme and state that you would like to use the Newingham Leisure and Youth Centre.
   (*a*) Refer to the Professor's questionnaire and ask permission for this to be distributed to members between the ages of 14 and 20 for their completion and for them to take part of the questionnaire home for completion by the adults.
   (*b*) Ask permission to use the premises for filming and for permission to invite the co-operation of the Principal of the centre.

Assignment No. 36

See Assignment Nos. 34 and 35.

Permission has been given to work on the series of programmes referred to in Assignments 34 and 35. The County Education Officer of Hopeshire has given approval for the circulation of the questionnaire and, subject to the County Council's consent, for the premises to be used for televising purposes. He does not foresee any objections but a fee will have to be paid for the use of the premises. He enclosed an application form. He suggested that SEAR make contact with the Centre. The small production committee has also had another meeting.

Mrs. Prober has now asked you to do the following:

1. Prepare a letter to be sent to Mr. M. Arnold, the Principal of Newingham Leisure and Youth Centre. Refer to the County Education Officer's letter and to the proposed series of programmes.
   (*a*) Enclose a copy of the questionnaire. SEAR would like Club members to complete Part I on the premises. Part II should be taken home for completion by parents/grandparents and returned the following week. If he agrees SEAR will send enough to provide one set for each member in 14–20 range. Ask for number required.
   (*b*) County Education Officer has provisionally agreed to filming. Ask permission for cameramen (names) to make a preliminary

survey and take some shots of premises (**no** individuals this time). Refer especially to theatre.

(*c*) Ask his advice about 'composite' families. You require about thirty. Should be drawn from club members. Ask for balance, Instruct that no communication be made by him to families. SEAR will make contact when names and addresses are received.

(*d*) Give him first provisional date for filming – six months away.

2. Send internal memo to SEAR printing department and copy of questionnaire. Ask for 1,000 copies – ask for printing cost estimate for programme budget account.
3. Draft a suitable letter that will be sent to parents and grandparents of thirty families chosen to invite them to a meeting at which the scheme will be fully explained and their participation invited. Do not say who gave their names. Refer to scheme in not more than one paragraph. With the letter should be included a reply sheet to include YES/NO response and names and address(es) of: (*a*) young people 10 or over; (*b*) parents; (*c*) grandparents, who will be attending the meeting. Reply is to be posted in enclosed envelope for which no postage will be required.

Assignment No. 37

The management of Newtown Aero and Marine Spares Ltd., a small engineering company manufacturing smaller parts required for aircraft and shipping, encountered difficulties in disposing of waste products, especially scrap metal and plastic. One day the general manager found the following in the suggestion box.

'*Sir, My two sons watched the new series on National Television, "Michael and the VIC's". The first programme was shown on Tuesday. The two boys sat spellbound. Next Tuesday cannot come soon enough. They both said they wished they could get a Super Ultralux for themselves. We have lots of waste. Could we make some models of this new spacecraft? I am sure they would sell.*' John Sellerton.

The general manager sent for the production manager and showed him the letter and asked if anything could be done.

P.M. I have never heard of 'Michael and the VIC's'.

G.M. Let me introduce you. I hadn't but I soon made it my business to find out. It is a new series. Michael is the new star, a young, gallant earthman ever ready to dart out into space to curb the activities of astro-tyrants, relieve beleaguered planets and destroy destructive machinery. He is accompanied by Karena and Serena, two beautiful and brave members of the Interstellar Vixen Invicta Corps, called VIC for short. They travel in a space vehicle – it looks like one of the world's fastest cars attached to a super space cone. This machine, the Super Ultralux, will take them into the remotest parts of space in pursuit of their enemies and villains. Their adventures will be even more exciting than anything we have ever seen on our screens. There are some pictures in the National Broadcasts Weekly.

P.M. Yes – we shall have a go to produce these. I think you ought to contact the National Television at once and secure the rights to copy the material and use the names, especially Super Ultralux, Michael and the VIC's, Michael, Karena, Serena.

G.M. I will get that set in motion at once. When can we have the first models?

P.M. The first prototypes will be ready by the end of the week – a one metre model of Super Ultralux and a six inch model. I will get Plastics to produce Michael, Karena and Serena, all fully equipped and able to fit into the one metre model. They will probably have a kit of replacement uniforms and dresses. This is fortunate as we are short on shipping orders at the moment.

Secretary. Excuse me, sir, but do you know that there is the International Toy Fair at Birmingham in six weeks?

G.M. You're wonderful, Moira. (To P.M.) Can we make it?

P.M. Yes – if you like the models we produce, we can become the centre of attention.

G.M. I will contact the Fair management.

After this meeting, you as Secretary, are given a number of tasks.

1. Produce for the General Manager and Production Manager a summarised account of this conversation. Present it so that each can readily see what he has to do.
2. Write to the Legal Department, National Television. Outline our plans and ask for the authority to copy material and use names in the programme. Please stress that we would like the sole rights as far as the manufacture of toys is concerned.
3. Write to the Organiser, International Toy Fair, Birmingham – we want a large, central display area. Ask for details, costs.

A week later the promised models appear – three of each. The production manager suggests that two of each are given to John Sellerton – one for each boy. The production manager apologises, 'I hope you do not mind that I have gone beyond your instructions – the section has produced 500 of each already – and we can go into production at once. We shall need special packing boxes and leaflets.'

The National Television has replied giving permission, subject to payment of royalty fees in respect of each item produced and for use of trade names, 'Michael and the VIC's', 'Super Ultralux', 'Vixen Invicta Corps' and the three names in association with the programme. An invoice for £450 was included.

A reply from the International Toy Fair indicated that space was still available – 30 m by 50 m. A booking form was enclosed.

The general manager now gives you extra tasks.

4. He has called a special meeting of the Board of Directors. He wants each member to have a memorandum about the new activities of the company. Will you do it for him?
5. Send a memo to the firm's display and design department. The following are required: design for special label 1 m by $\frac{1}{2}$ m for the boxes containing the large toy Super Ultralux; production of all the display material for the International Toy Fair – give them the necessary information.
6. Letter to John Sellerton – to thank him for the suggestion. Enclose cheque for £25.
7. Letter to his sons to invite them to meet the Managing Director – give time and date. To be received by Secretary. Mother may come – father can have time off. Toys will be presented (do not tell them).
8. Memo to production to arrange for boys to have a tour of factory and premises.
9. Reply to National Television. Cheque to be sent. Ask if 'Michael of the Screen' could come to Birmingham one day – to autograph boxes containing models (Michael's name is John Plautus).
10. When reply has been received from National Television, send completed form to Birmingham. Also mention that 'Michael of the Screen' will be there on the Friday from 10 to 6. Ask if facilities exist for entertainment of V.I.P.s. Inform display and design department and ask them to give urgent attention to preparation for the Toy Fair.
11. Send memo to all sections involved and ask for breakdown of costs so that toys can be priced.

Assignment No. 38

See Assignment No. 37.

Newtown Aero and Marine Spares Ltd. has found that its new project centred around the National Television series 'Michael and the VIC's' has been a great success. Demands for the toys and models associated with it are pouring in, not only from Britain but also from other countries. Wholesalers, shopkeepers and the public are asking if it intends to extend its range. Simultaneously with all this has been an improvement in trade for the main business.

A meeting of directors was held to consider the developments and it was agreed:

1. to seek additional accommodation so that the toy production side could be further developed;

2. to create a subsidiary company which would handle all the toy business.

The general manager has asked you to prepare for him a letter to be sent to The Estates Controller, Northdown. This letter should summarise developments that have taken place and indicate the company's interest in establishing a factory in Northdown, which is one of the more recent New Towns. Ask for information about Northdown generally and literature concerning the industrial sites available. The general manager would like to visit Northdown and meet the Estate Controller at a time convenient to the latter.

He would also like you to prepare a notice to be given to all employees to inform them of the Board's plans and to ask that any who might be interested in a transfer to let him know. Prepare a reply slip. It should be emphasised that a favourable reply does not commit anyone. At a later stage an opportunity will be given for a definite option.

A memorandum should be drawn up for submission to the department for registering new companies. Outline what has taken place. The directors' resolution should be quoted. The new company's registered office will be at Newtown, but the main factory will be at Northdown. The directors have decided that the company should be called Michael-Vic Toys. Ask for provisional approval of the name and request the necessary forms and instructions of procedure.

Assignment No. 39

It is now the third week of the new session at Oldchester College of Further Education. The hours are from 9.00 a.m. to 1.00 p.m. and 2.00 p.m. to 4.30 p.m. The Principal has noticed that some students have been arriving at varying times after 9.15 a.m. Others have been leaving as early as 3.30 p.m.

(i) As his secretary, you have been asked to prepare a memorandum to be sent to each Head of Department. Students are to be reminded of college times. They must be in class on time. There is to be no early leaving. Exceptionally – Head may give permission to leave early – he should give them a signed note. Give Heads times of trains and buses.

The following information is from time-tables. Trains – from North – arrive at Oldchester Station – 7.40 a.m., 8.10 a.m., 8.40 a.m. From South – arrive at 7.37 a.m., 8.07 a.m., 8.37 a.m. 5 minutes' walk from station. Buses: Route 77 – 8.20 a.m., 8.35 a.m., 8.50 a.m. Route 111 – 8.28 a.m., 8.53 a.m. Route 114 – 8.51 a.m., stop outside College from Bordertown direction. Route 77 – 8.25 a.m., 8.40 a.m., 8.55 a.m. Route 111 – 8.13 a.m., 8.43 a.m. Route 114 – 8.55 a.m. – stop on opposite side of road from Seaville.

Evening. Railway – trains to North 4.45 p.m., 5.15 p.m., 5.45 p.m. To South 4.40 p.m., 5.10 p.m., 5.40 p.m. Buses – Route 77 – buses every 15 mins: Route 111 – buses every half-hour from 4.40 p.m. Route 114 – every half-hour from 4.50 p.m.

(ii) The Principal has also asked you to prepare a notice, to be duplicated, to be displayed in classrooms, common rooms, refectories and halls. Instructions for students. Also add break times – morning 10.30 a.m. to 10.45 a.m. – afternoon 3.00 p.m. to 3.15 p.m.

(iii) Prepare a suitable outline permit for students to leave early. It should provide for Name, Department, Course, Day and Time of Leaving. Signature by Head of Department.

(iv) The Principal has received the following letter from a parent.

10 Sandham Lane,
Old Nutbury,
nr., Nutwell

5th October, 1980

The Principal,
Oldchester College of Further Education,
Oldchester,
OL6 7HP.

Dear Sir,

My daughter, Anna, has informed me that she has been reprimanded for late arrival at College.

We live in the small village of Old Nutbury, about 10 miles from Nutwell. The first bus into Nutwell leaves here at 8.25 a.m. and arrives at 8.40 a.m., if it is on time. The first available train to Oldchester is at 8.55 a.m. This does not arrive till 9.40 a.m.

I should be very pleased if you would excuse her if she does not arrive at College until after that.

Yours faithfully,
J. T. Shepherd.

He has asked you to do the following. Check with the Divisional Education Office – a school bus might be available. If so, arrange for Anna to catch this. If not, write letter giving permission.

You ring the D.E.O. A bus runs to Oldchester and can be diverted to pick Anna up at Old Nutbury at 8.00 a.m. – outside her home. It leaves Oldchester at 4.25 p.m. and will stop outside the College. If she has her bus pass/season ticket she should surrender these at the College office. No charge will be made for travel on the school bus.

Prepare the letter of reply for signature.

Assignment No. 40

You are the Secretary to Mr. J. Moneyman, the Manager of the Oldchester Branch of the Bank of Great Britain. The following letters have been received by him and passed to you to prepare replies.

Letter 1.

11 Cathedral Drive,
Oldchester,
Hopeshire.

March 18th, 1980

Dear Sir,

I am 21 years of age and am planning to get married in April, 1981. My fiancee and I would like to buy our own house and would like your advice about paying for one. I am a research assistant with good prospects for the future.

Yours faithfully,
J. W. Treadwell.

Letter 2.

'Highview',
Tanners Lane,
Oldchester,
Hopeshire.

March 19th, 1980

The Manager,
Bank of Great Britain,
Oldchester Branch,
Market Road,
Oldchester.

Dear Sir,

My parents emigrated to Canada ten years ago to be close to my sister. My father has now retired from work and is drawing a small pension. As they have no other source of income I would like to send them forty pounds each month. Would you tell me if I am allowed to do this and, if so, how should I go about it?

Yours sincerely,
Michael Vicarson.

Letter 3.

4, Brightmans Crescent,
Oldchester,
Hopeshire.

March 18th, 1980

Mr. J. Moneyman,
Bank of Great Britain,
Market Road,
Oldchester,
Hopeshire.

Dear Mr. Moneyman,

I passed my driving test today and I want to get a car as soon as possible. I have seen one I want. It is a red Capri, about five years old, a 1600. It's a fine model and only costs £1000. I have saved about £100 and would like to borrow the rest. Can I get a loan from the bank? If not, is there some other way I can raise the money?

Please reply as soon as possible.

Yours sincerely,
Peter Moonman.

P.S. Do I have any other costs to pay?

Bank manager's notes

Letter 1. Acknowledge. Normal to get a mortgage from Building Society or Insurance Company. Borrower will be asked to provide at least 5% of cost of house as a deposit (e.g. £20,000 house – deposit at least £1,000). First – save for deposit. Repayment mortgage spread over a number of years. Interest also to be paid. Can save through Bdg Socy/Insurance Co/Bank. Tax relief on mortgage interest. Quite frequent to assist repayment with aid of endowment policies – which give protection in event of death before repayments finished. See leaflet 'Insurance to Buy Your Home'. Enclose copy.

J. W. Treadwell seems to be first-time buyer. Special government help. See Dept. of Environment leaflet 'Homeloan'. Copy to be enclosed. Tell him about bank's Insurance Advisory Dept. Suggest he ring for an appointment with that dept.

Letter 4.

'Happy Home',
46 Deacon Crescent,
Oldchester,
Hopeshire.

March 18th, 1980

Mr. J. Moneyman,
Bank Manager,
Bank of Great Britain,
Market Road,
Oldchester.

Dear Mr. Moneyman,

I am fifty-five years of age, with a wife and two sons and two daughters, all married. I own my own house, have a caravan in the South of England and have shares to the value of £9,000. There is also other valuable property.

My wife is about my age but does not understand much about property and the other matters. She will be hopeless at trying to sort things out if I die suddenly. I do not trust the children, for I am sure they will each try to look after their own interests and my wife may finish up with nothing. A friend has told me I ought to make a will. When I told him all about my problems he said that I ought to write to my bank manager.

Can you help me?

Yours sincerely,
James K. Leedman.

Letter 2. Can be sent (i) by Banker's Order. Bank will arrange transfer – but must know – father's name and address – which Canadian bank (Branch? Account number?); (ii) by Bank of Great Britain Money Order – in sterling, American Dollars, Canadian Dollars. Buyer must post it – father to find bank to accept. List of banks can be obtained; (iii) by customer's own cheque, payable in Canadian Dollars or sterling. Handling charge payable. Reminder – must comply with U.K. Currency Export Regulations.

Letter 3. Send him 'Handyloan' pamphlet. Explain – government rules for loan for cars. Borrower must find one-third cost. Remainder to be paid over 24 mths. at longest. He could have to find another £233. Loan would be £670. Over 2 yrs. Repayments £32.96 per month. Over 1 year £60.94 per mth. – these include interest. Bank will decide on loan when form completed. Other ways of raising money – hire purchase.

Other costs: car tax; insurance; especially fully comprehensive – if he is under 25 it could be high. An older car – maintenance costs could be high.

Letter 4. Thank writer for letter. This is a delicate situation – a tactful letter is called for. The bank can help through its trust department. Suggest that Mr. Leedman call to see me – a suitable date can be selected from my diary. Before date is given contact Trustees department and arrange for someone to come to the branch. Let Mr. Leedman know he will be there. Enclose a copy of the leaflets – 'What our trustee department does' and 'Making a Will'.

Assignment No. 41

The Autumn term meeting of the Governors of Newtown College of Further Education is to be held on October 31, 1980. The Principal has asked the Head of Department of Business and Secretarial Studies for a report on his department. He has made the following notes and wishes you to prepare a formal report to be presented by him. All the information should be set out so that it can be readily followed.

1. Enrolments at Sept 30. Full-time day. G.C.E. 'A' Level – 52 students. Subjects – English Literature, History, French, Geography, Sociology, Philosophy. No subject with less than 16 students. G.C.E. 'O' Level – Eng. Lang. 49, Eng. Lit. 30, Mod. Hist. 32, Maths. 28, French 25, Spanish 23, Sociology 18, Drama 20. G.C.E. Business 'A' Level – 45 students – Subjects – Accounts, Stats, Economics, Law, Computer Studies. G.C.E. 'O' Level (Business) – Economics 23, English (Business and Professional) 22, Stats 23, Accounts 23, Law 23. Part-time day 'O' Level course 18 students taking English Lang., Maths, History, Economics, Accounts. F.T. B.E.C. General Course 24: B.E.C. Year 1–26, Year 2, 22. Part-time B.E.C. General 18, National Year 1 – 17, Year 2 – 15. Secretarial 80 students to study Typing, Shorthand, Shorthand/Typing, Audio Typing, Office Practice. To take Sec. Studies Cert, London Chamber of Commerce and R.S.A. Single Subjects. 33 to take the London Chamber of Commerce Private Secretaries Cert. 35 the Private Secretaries Diploma. Evening classes – enrolments for classes running. A.L. English Literature 22, A.L. Modern History 21, A.L. Sociology 17, A.L. French 17, A.L. Economics 18, A.L. Accounts 21, A.L. Law 26. O.L. English Language 51 – 2 classes, O.L. Economics 22, O.L. Accounts 30, O.L. Law 23, O.L. Eng. Lit. 17. Typewriting: Beginners 18, Intermediate 16, Advanced 16, Shorthand: Beginners 17,

Intermediate 16. Institute of Accounting Staff 21. Institute of Travel Agents 17.

2. Staffing. The following full-time staff have been appointed – Mrs. S. Champion, Secretarial; Mr. T. Ovenall, Sociology; Mr. P. Slowcombe, English/History.
3. Work Experience Day Release – arrangements for all Secretarial students to have 1 day per week in local offices. All Bus. Studs/Admin – work experience to be found by County Hall, District Council, Electricity Board, Forestry Commission in Hopeshire. Last year – Sec. arrangements very successful. New scheme for Bus. Studies/Admin students.
4. Drama tutor – to produce for Easter – 'The Tempest' – 1 week of performances
5. Exam results – duplicated – set given as appendix. G.C.E. results all very pleasing. Note in 'A' Level a total of 30 grade 'A'. 'O' Levels – 70 grade 'A'. Secretarial: Private Secretary's Certificate and Diploma Examinations – all passed. 75% gained distinctions. Last year the first B.E.C. General Courses – and B.E.C. National Courses which involve integrated subject studies and team teaching. Success in General and in the first year National shows college on right path.
6. Ten students placed in Universities – 16 in Polytechnics. **No** leaver failed to get employment.
7. Negotiations to start TOPS course in Secretarial Studies and Legal Executives. Expected start in Jan 81.

Assignment No. 42

The management of Newtown Electronics has received the following note in the staff suggestions box: 'For the third time this year a national strike has prevented me from getting petrol for my car. This firm makes some wonderful gadgets. Can't we produce a new kind of car that doesn't run on petrol? I saw a programme about using the sun's energy to heat houses. Can't we use it to run a car? – Signed by S. Sunwell.'

The general manager asked you, his secretary,

1. to reply to S. Sunwell. Acknowledge and thank him for his letter. A useful idea – it will be considered. Enclose a cheque of £5 for the idea;
2. to send a memo to the Research Department – ask that the idea be seriously considered. Enclose a copy of the suggestion. Suggest they bring forward ideas about Solar Research. Any work done to be treated as very confidential. Request that Chief Research Officer meet the general manager.

This meeting took place the following day, June 16th, 1981. The conversation below took place and was taken down by you.

G.M. Hello, Lloyd; I hope that you have had a few minutes to think about this.

C.R.O. Yes. I must say that I have never seen myself as being part of the car manufacturing industry. It's so different from calculators, tape recorders and most electronic products.

G.M. True, but there's always a chance to start something new. Have you any ideas?

C.R.O. Yes. One or two scientific journals have suggested tapping the sun's energy as the vehicle moves. I think this could be very limiting and very expensive. It would not work at night. From what I have read some very heavy equipment would have to be fixed on top of the car. It would be a long time before people would want to buy one.

G.M. What next?

C.R.O. I think we ought to go in for some more general solar research first. I have been interesting myself in this for some time and have read most of the recent reports and accounts about the subject.

G.M. That sounds interesting. Carry on.

C.R.O. In the field of optics the sun's light is being used to help operate some electronic gadgets. We could experiment in this field. We could also try to produce solar batteries.

G.M. How would you do that?

C.R.O. By making a suntrap building which would utilise the energy from light and the energy waves at either end of the spectrum. The energy would be built up in storage receivers and could be used whenever we want to charge the solar batteries. These would be similar to ordinary batteries.

G.M. Do you think we ought to go further into this?

C.R.O. I will trace all the research that has been going on in the universities and at those industrial laboratories that have released information. From what I discover I will work out a plan of action. While this is coming in we could make a start by setting aside a space for a solar laboratory. I think I have enough basic material on which to work.

G.M. What do you want, then?

C.R.O. An upstairs room with a ceiling that opens to the sky. If you can clear it, the upstairs records room will be ideal.

G.M. I will get admin. to move the records. There is basement space available. Building maintenance can carry out any preliminary construction work. I will ask them to put 'No Admittance' notices on the doors. Do you want any security support?

C.R.O. One or two men at the entrance to the room. The staff involved should be issued with special passes. Could I have Michael Keene to work with me? He is an electronics engineer with experience of the motor industry. He has done a study on 'Heat Engines' and has recently done some work on his house so that he can use solar power for his central heating system. He will also be able to advise on aspects of the safety and health at work regulations.

G.M. Yes. You can have him. Let me know the names of any others that you require. I would like a special budget estimate for this to cover the next six months.

Will you prepare a summary of the main points of this conversation? It should be marked 'Very Confidential'. One for the general manager and one for the C.R.O. Your file copy and these notes will be kept in the company's confidential file safe.

Prepare for the general manager memoranda to the administration manager and the supervisor of Building Maintenance to implement the decisions that have been taken so far.

Write a letter to the Hopeshire Security Services asking for two more security men for the part of the building to be used for this project.

The Chief Research Officer wants you to draft a letter that can be used to send to the universities to ask for information about any research work being done on solar energy. It will be addressed to 'The Dean of the Faculty of Science and Engineering of. . . .' A similar letter should be prepared to be sent to the Chief Research Officer of any industrial organisations that might have information.

Send a memo to the company's printing section requesting ten special pass cards – orange colour – space for photographs – name – 'admit . . . to the Long Room' – date – signature of general manager – signature of holder.

Note – no reference should be made to any of the proposals raised in this conversation when preparing memoranda or letters.

Assignment No. 43

Approval has been given for the construction of the new motorway, the M148, which will run through Hopeshire to give access to Newtown, Oldchester and Oldville. It is reported that Buildwell Constructions will be starting work on the site at the Newtown end in three months. The secretary of the Hopeshire Archaeological Society overhears some colleagues discussing the project and the proposed dates. At a recent archaeological conference he has heard that the Romans were very active in the area around Oldchester and Oldville. Professor James Spading expressed the view that a road ran between the two modern towns and that a settlement might be found.

The Secretary, James Fithly, called an emergency meeting of the committee. There he revealed what he had learned of the archaeological possibilities of the area and of the imminence of excavation work on the motorway area. After some excited discussion it was decided that the secretary should:

1. contact the Newtown Flying Club and enquire if there is someone who could help to arrange an aerial photographic reconnaissance of the area. This would involve taking a number of photographs and examining them to see if the fields revealed signs of earlier occupation;
2. write to the contractors to ask their help. The group would like freedom to explore the area to be excavated and carry out as thorough an archaeological survey as time would allow;
3. write to the Department of the Environment to seek advice and help.

The Flying Club replied. The chairman, Group Captain E. Ironside, volunteered his services – both plane and a photographer. He invited the archaeological society to nominate one or two people to join him and act as advisers on the flights.

The contractors pointed out that they were tied to a time-table by the Department of the Environment. They did not anticipate starting in the area under question for at least six months. The managing director had instructed the Motorway Construction Supervisor to put a mechanical digger in the area to enable the approved surface to be lifted. The Society would then be free to do such archaeological work as it wished until asked to withdraw.

Also – archaeological teams were free to work for six weeks on the Newtown stretch while the rest of that site was being prepared.

The Department of the Environment replied. The Roads and Motorways Section – contractors were being encouraged to co-operate. The Ancient Monuments Section – very interested. Asking their Roman Antiquities adviser, Dr. Alan Mole, to contact the Society. He would give advice – and, if wanted, secure the services of other archaeological groups.

Later, Dr. Mole wrote – expressed interest. Would like to meet Society – would give talk on 'Romans and Hopeshire'. In it he would offer suggestions on what to look for. Suggested a date in two weeks. Would like report on all activities. Finds should be reported to Curator, Newtown Museum, or to Curator, Oldchester Castle Museum.

Secretary of Hopeshire Archaeological Society replied to:

1. Flying Club – thanks – appreciation. Committee nominated himself and Dr. Joneswell, an archaeologist from Oldchester. Asked Gp. Capt. to phone him at Newtown 688668 to fix date and time.
2. contractors – very pleased. Hopeshire Society ready to start at once. Promise of assistance from Institute of Archaeology. Looking forward to Dr. Mole's advice from Department of Environment. Would they suggest a person with whom they could liaise?

3. Department of the Environment – to each section. An appropriate letter of thanks. In section looked forward to co-operation with Dr. Mole.
4. Dr. Mole – thanks. Would be delighted for his talk. Accepted his date – members would be there. Indicate action taken by Society so far. Promise to co-operate as suggested.

Assume that you are the personal secretary of the people involved or, if this seems impractical, the person himself. Prepare all the correspondence referred to in this assignment.

Assignment No. 44

The Headmaster of Oldville Comprehensive School has agreed that a party of fifth- and sixth-formers should spend two weeks in France during the early part of the Summer Term. The staff concerned have proposed that the party stay at the Centre International, just outside Montauban in the South of France. The Centre belongs to the University of the South of France and is used by parties of students engaged in various types of field studies. There is a domestic staff to provide catering facilities and look after the property. The Centre is made available in May to students from outside France.

The Headmaster has asked you, the School Secretary, to deal with all the paper work involved.

Your first task is to write to the Residential Warden, M. Jean Dubois, to ask if the Centre is available from May 7th to May 21st, 1980. Mr. Stephen Lingfield, the Senior Languages Master, estimates that there will be 15 boys, 15 girls, 3 masters and 3 mistresses. If it is possible make a provisional booking. Ask for a scale of charges and any literature, descriptive of the Centre or the area, that might be available.

A letter should be written to the Southern Region of British Rail asking for details of fares – from Victoria to Montauban. Try also Victoria to French north coastal port – with costs for a 40-seater coach. Ask also details about time-tables.

The two letters are to be sent in November.

The replies to these two letters have been received. The Centre is available for the period in question. Enquiries by phone have shown that Hopeshire County Education Authority's 40-seater coach is available from May 5th to 23rd and that a driver will go with it. A comparison of charges has led to a decision to use the coach, take it over on the ferry to Dieppe and drive to the Centre. An overnight stay will be necessary on the outward and return journeys.

The education authority will agree to the visit in term time if those organising the journey can offer a programme of activities that is sufficiently educational. These proposals have been made and provisionally agreed. During the two weeks away the party will undertake a survey of Montauban and District. There will be five study groups – for geography, history of the area, how the people earn their living, social life and education. Each group will be advised by a teacher and led by a sixth-form student studying 'A' Level French. He/she will act as the group interpreter. Two pupils will be appointed as official photographers. Any who are artists may provide sketches of buildings, scenes and local people as required by any of the groups.

The estimated cost for the visit will be £60.

Mr. Lingfield has now asked you to prepare a letter/leaflet to be sent to the parents of fifth- and sixth-formers to outline in general terms the nature of the holiday and to offer them enough information to help them to decide whether or not their son/daughter will join the party. This leaflet should provide a tear-off slip that each parent may return.

When the slips have been returned and the composition of the party is known another letter should be prepared, addressed to the parents, but with a copy for each of the pupils who will be going. This should elaborate on the proposed survey. To the above information should be added that each group will be expected to submit a written report. All the reports will be bound together – any other material (such as photographs, sketches, tickets) will be included. The school's printing section will be asked to print the material later. Also deal with passports, currency and suggestions for kit to be taken. Each should have best wear – general activity clothing – pyjamas – towels– washing materials. Writing materials – ruler – binoculars – camera. Ask pupils to complete a form showing group preferences (in order of merit) and indicate if they wish to be considered as artists or photographers for the group.

Three visits will be arranged – one to the mountains, one to a coastal town and one to an industrial centre. Food and transport included in the cost.

Another letter will be issued to give travel instructions. The letter now being sent should set out arrangements for payment – immediate initial deposit. Remainder by 19th April. May be paid in instalments. You will receive all payments at the office.

Send a letter to the Centre to confirm booking – enclose a deposit of £10 for each person (to be converted to French Francs and paid by cheque). Final numbers – 15 boys, 17 girls. Four staff – 2 m – 2 f. In charge – Mr. Stephen Lingfield. His home address – 1 Chaucer Close, Oldville, Hopeshire.

For the Headmaster prepare a letter to the County Education Office. It should outline the proposals for the trip and request the Education Committee's approval, name the four members of staff and ask for leave of absence with pay for them for the period mentioned, submit the list of the names and addresses of the pupils going (to be a separate enclosure) and request permission for the hire of the bus and driver (indicate that a form of application has been completed and is attached). This should reach the County offices by the second Tuesday in April.

Index

In this index the figures in the medium type refer to the pages in parts 1 & 2 in which the topic is discussed; those in bold type refer to those assignments in which the topic appears as an activity for the student.

Abstract, 64

Catalogue, preparation, **7**
Charts, 64–8: **7, 15**
Comprehension, basic, 41–2

Diagrams, 64–8
Digest, 63

Forms, 67, 69–74: **23, 28, 30**

Invitations, **14, 27**
Invoice, **11**

Letter
  giving information, 16–18: **1, 8, 11, 13, 14, 15, 17, 22, 27, 29, 32, 35, 36**
  giving instructions, 22–3: **6, 11, 13, 17, 23, 28, 29, 33, 34**
  invitations, **14, 36, 37**
  layout, 12–15
  ordering goods or asking for services, 18–22: **1, 14, 19, 24, 27, 35, 36, 37, 38, 42, 43, 44**
  praise or complaint, 23–9: **3, 4, 6, 8, 11, 12, 13, 14, 15, 25, 26, 29, 33, 43**
  replying to correspondence, 29–32: **3, 4, 6, 12, 13, 15, 24, 25, 26, 30, 32, 33, 37, 39, 40, 42, 43**
  seeking information, 15–16: **13, 14, 15, 19, 22, 25, 43, 44**
  sympathy, **17**
Lists, **1, 18**

Meetings
  minutes of, 49–54: **29**
  notice of and agenda, 45–9: **28, 32**
Memo, 1–4: **2, 3, 18, 20, 21, 36, 37, 42**
Memoranda, 8–12: **8, 9, 17, 18, 20, 21, 23, 27, 31, 34, 35, 37, 38, 42**

Note-taking, 43–4: **4**
Notices, 4–8: **2, 14, 17, 18, 19, 20, 21, 24, 27, 28, 31, 38, 39**

Questionnaires, 67, 69, 74–8: **34**

Reporting
  note-taking, 43–44
  verbatim, 42–3
Reports, 37–40: **5, 12, 17, 18, 19, 22, 25, 41**
Reports, statements, **4, 12, 22, 35**

Summary
  correspondence, 55–9: **26, 32**
  note-form, 59–63: **8, 19, 21, 23, 32, 35, 37, 42**
Synopsis, 63: **19**

Telegrams, 32–4
Telex, 35–7: **5, 6, 10, 14, 16, 17, 26**